Better Homes and Gardens®

fresh and simple™

cooking
for friends

Better Homes and Gardens® Books

Des Moines, Iowa

All of us at Better Homes and Gardens® Books are dedicated to providing you with the information and ideas you need to create delicious foods. We welcome your comments and suggestions. Write to us at: Better Homes and Gardens® Books, Cookbook Editorial Department, 1716 Locust St., Des Moines, IA 50309–3023.

If you would like to purchase additional copies of any of our books, check with your local bookstore.

Our seal assures you that every recipe in *Cooking for Friends* has been tested in the Better Homes and Gardens® Test Kitchen. This means that each recipe is practical and reliable, and meets our high standards of taste appeal. We guarantee your satisfaction with this book for as long as you own it.

Pictured on front cover: Thai Shrimp & Fresh Vegetable Rice (see recipe, *page 49*)
Pictured on page 1: Wild Mushroom Ravioli with Sage Butter (see recipe, *page 51*)

Better Homes and Gardens® Books
An imprint of Meredith® Books

Fresh and Simple™ *Cooking for Friends*
Editor: Lisa Holderness
Project Editor and Writer: Lisa Kingsley
Contributing Editors: Pam Anderson, Nancy Verde Barr, Jennifer Darling, Janet Pittman, Spectrum Communications Services, Inc.
Designer: Craig Hanken
Copy Chief: Catherine Hamrick
Copy and Production Editor: Terri Fredrickson
Contributing Copy Editor: Martha Coloff Long
Contributing Proofreaders: Sheila Mauck, Mary Pas
Electronic Production Coordinator: Paula Forest
Editorial and Design Assistants: Judy Bailey, Treesa Landry, Karen Schirm
Test Kitchen Director: Sharon Stilwell
Test Kitchen Product Supervisor: Marilyn Cornelius
Food Stylists: Lynn Blanchard, Janet Pittman
Photography: Jim Krantz, Kritsada Panichgul
Prop Stylist: Karen Johnson
Production Director: Douglas M. Johnston
Production Manager: Pam Kvitne
Assistant Prepress Manager: Marjorie J. Schenkelberg

Meredith® Books
Editor in Chief: James D. Blume
Design Director: Matt Strelecki
Managing Editor: Gregory H. Kayko

Director, Sales & Marketing, Retail: Michael A. Peterson
Director, Sales & Marketing, Special Markets: Rita McMullen
Director, Sales & Marketing, Home & Garden Center Channel: Ray Wolf
Director, Operations: George A. Susral

Vice President, General Manager: Jamie L. Martin

Better Homes and Gardens® Magazine
Editor in Chief: Jean LemMon
Executive Food Editor: Nancy Byal

Meredith Publishing Group
President, Publishing Group: Christopher M. Little
Vice President, Consumer Marketing & Development: Hal Oringer

Meredith Corporation
Chairman and Chief Executive Officer: William T. Kerr

Chairman of the Executive Committee: E. T. Meredith III

contents

company? tonight? go for it!

Do your social life a favor: Invite friends over—even on the spur of the moment. The flavorful, innovative fare in *Cooking for Friends,* part of the *Better Homes and Gardens® Fresh & Simple™* series, is worthy of company but simple enough for weeknight get-togethers. What's more, these recipes call for fresh, readily available ingredients, so you won't waste time searching for obscure items at the market or cooking for hours. You can make any of these recipes in about 30 minutes! So relax and savor a couple of laid-back hours with friends.

first
bites

fruited cheese spirals

Finger food gets a fresh new look! Dried fruit adds jewel tones to these clever spirals filled with prosciutto, cream cheese, and the cinnamon-pepper flavor of fresh basil.

Prep: 10 minutes Stand: 15 minutes Chill: 4 hours
Makes about 24 servings

In a small saucepan bring the orange juice or apple juice to boiling. Stir in dried fruit; remove from heat. Let stand, covered, about 15 minutes or until fruit is softened. Drain. Meanwhile, in a medium bowl stir together cream cheese, sour cream or yogurt, and the ¼ cup basil.

Spread cream cheese mixture evenly over one side of each cracker bread or tortilla. Sprinkle each with the softened fruit. Place some of the prosciutto or ham near an edge of each round. Tightly roll up, beginning with edge closest to meat. Wrap each roll in plastic wrap and refrigerate for 4 to 24 hours.

To serve, cut each roll into 1-inch-thick slices. If desired, garnish with basil leaves and orange slices.

Nutrition facts per serving: 115 cal., 6 g total fat (2 g sat. fat), 12 mg chol., 142 mg sodium, 14 g carbo., 0 g fiber, 3 g pro. Daily values: 5% vit. A, 4% vit. C, 1% calcium, 2% iron

½ cup orange juice or apple juice

1 cup dried fruit (such as cranberries, snipped cherries, and/or snipped apricots)

1 8-ounce tub cream cheese

½ cup dairy sour cream or plain yogurt

¼ cup fresh basil leaves, finely snipped

2 14- to 15-inch soft cracker bread rounds or four 7- to 8-inch flour tortillas

4 very thin slices prosciutto or cooked ham

Fresh basil leaves (optional)

Orange slices (optional)

white bean dip with toasted pita chips

Almost everybody loves Mediterranean—and this creamy, aromatic dip is the essence of it. Inspired by hummus and *skordalia*, a Greek puree of potatoes, garlic, and almonds, it spices up predictable breads and crudités.

¼ **cup soft bread crumbs**

2 **tablespoons dry white wine or water**

1 **15- to 19-ounce can cannellini beans or great northern beans, rinsed and drained**

¼ **cup slivered almonds, toasted**

3 **cloves garlic, minced**

2 **tablespoons lemon juice**

2 **tablespoons olive oil**

¼ **teaspoon salt**

⅛ **teaspoon ground red pepper**

2 **teaspoons snipped fresh oregano or basil**

1 **recipe Toasted Pita Chips**

1 **red and/or yellow sweet pepper, cut into 1-inch-wide strips (optional)**

Prep: 20 minutes Bake: 12 minutes   Makes 30 servings

In a small bowl combine bread crumbs and wine or water; set aside. In a food processor bowl or blender container combine beans, almonds, garlic, lemon juice, olive oil, salt, and ground red pepper. Cover and process until almost smooth. Add bread-crumb mixture. Cover and process until smooth. Stir in the oregano or basil. If desired, cover dip and refrigerate for 3 to 24 hours to blend flavors.

Serve with Toasted Pita Chips and, if desired, sweet pepper strips.

Toasted Pita Chips: Split 5 large pita bread rounds in half horizontally; cut each circle into 6 wedges (kitchen shears work well for this task). Place the wedges in a single layer on large baking sheets. Brush with 2 tablespoons olive oil or melted butter. If desired, sprinkle with paprika. Bake in a 350° oven for 12 to 15 minutes or until crisp and golden brown.

Nutrition facts per serving: 59 cal., 2 g total fat (0 g sat. fat), 0 mg chol., 96 mg sodium, 8 g carbo., 1 g fiber, 2 g pro. Daily values: 0% vit. A, 0% vit. C, 1% calcium, 3% iron

tomato & olive crostini

Italian cooks pull off appetizers with flair, even with basic ingredients. Just-from-the-garden herbs, plum tomatoes, and bold kalamata olives top these crisp, toasted rounds that would be delicious served alongside cubes of fresh mozzarella.

Prep: 20 minutes Bake: 8 minutes   Makes about 24 servings

In a small bowl combine tomatoes, olives, herb, vinegar, the 2 teaspoons oil, and the garlic. If desired, cover and refrigerate for up to 4 hours.

Cut bread into ½-inch-thick slices. Arrange bread on a baking sheet. Bake in a 400° oven for 3 to 4 minutes or until lightly browned. Turn slices over and lightly brush with the 2 tablespoons oil. Bake for 3 to 4 minutes or until edges are golden brown.

To serve, spoon the tomato mixture on the oiled side of the toast. Sprinkle with Parmesan cheese. Return to oven and bake for 2 to 3 minutes more or until cheese is melted.

Nutrition facts per serving: 50 cal., 3 g total fat (0 g sat. fat), 1 mg chol., 114 mg sodium, 6 g carbo., 0 g fiber, 1 g pro. Daily values: 0% vit. A, 3% vit. C, 1% calcium, 2% iron

1 cup chopped plum tomatoes

⅓ cup coarsely chopped pimiento-stuffed green olives

⅓ cup coarsely chopped pitted kalamata or ripe olives

2 tablespoons snipped fresh herb (such as oregano, marjoram, thyme, and/or rosemary)

1 tablespoon balsamic vinegar

2 teaspoons olive oil

1 teaspoon bottled minced garlic

1 8-ounce loaf baguette-style French bread

2 tablespoons olive oil

3 tablespoons shredded Parmesan cheese

here's to **crostini**

The French have canapés; the Italians have crostini. Crostini, or "little toasts," are perfect for celebrating friendship and good times. A bit like bruschetta in miniature, crostini are small, thin slices of toasted bread brushed with olive oil and crowned with fresh toppings. The possibilities are almost limitless. Some tasty choices include grilled zucchini marinated in balsamic vinegar, olive oil, and capers; roasted red peppers and fresh mozzarella; or caramelized onions and goat cheese or Gorgonzola.

baked kasseri
cheese spread

When chilly winds blow, cozy up to the fire and linger over a glass of red wine, a loaf of crusty bread, and this creamy spread of kasseri cheese, piquant olives, and oregano.

12 ounces kasseri* or
         scamorze cheese

⅔ cup kalamata olives, pitted and
       quartered

2 tablespoons snipped fresh oregano

1 clove garlic, minced

¼ teaspoon crushed red pepper

   French bread, apples,
      or crackers

Prep: 20 minutes Bake: 8 minutes   Makes 12 servings

Cut cheese into ½-inch-thick slices. Layer cheese in the bottom of a shallow 1-quart quiche dish or a 9-inch pie plate, overlapping if necessary. Toss together the olives, oregano, garlic, and red pepper. Sprinkle over the cheese.

Bake in a 450° oven for 8 to 10 minutes or until cheese just begins to melt. Serve immediately on bread, apples, or crackers; rewarm cheese as needed.

Nutrition facts per serving (spread only): 141 cal., 12 g total fat (7 g sat. fat), 30 mg chol., 350 mg sodium, 1 g carbo., 0 g fiber, 7 g pro. Daily values: 0% vit. A, 0% vit. C, 14% calcium, 0% iron

Note: Traditionally Greek, kasseri cheese is made with either sheep's or goat's milk. Its sharp, salty flavor and meltability make it a natural for this dish.

appetizing ideas
Even for the most casual get-togethers, it's nice to have an assortment of nibbles for your guests to enjoy as a prelude to the main event. But if you're planning a no-fuss evening, just make one simple starter from scratch. Then fill in with purchased crudités, bagel chips, tortilla chips with salsa, purchased hummus with warm wedges of pita bread, or marinated olives. Stylish but easy!

nachos de mer

If the Scandinavians had invented nachos, they might taste something like this. Reminiscent of the northlanders' famed open-faced sandwiches, toasted pita wedges are topped with a delicate seafood salad and crowned with fresh tomatoes.

1 recipe Toasted Pita Wedges

1 cup finely chopped, seeded plum tomatoes

⅓ cup finely chopped red or green sweet pepper

1½ cups chopped cooked shrimp or crabmeat

2 tablespoons mayonnaise or salad dressing

1 tablespoon finely chopped green onion

2 teaspoons Dijon-style mustard

1½ teaspoons snipped fresh dillweed

⅛ teaspoon salt

1½ cups shredded Havarti or Swiss cheese (6 ounces)

Prep: 25 minutes Bake: 13 minutes   Makes 18 servings

Prepare Toasted Pita Wedges. Set aside. In a small bowl combine tomatoes and sweet pepper. In a medium bowl combine shrimp or crabmeat, mayonnaise, green onion, mustard, dillweed, and salt. Stir in cheese. If desired, cover and refrigerate both mixtures for up to 4 hours.

To make nachos, place the pita wedges on 2 large baking sheets. Top with shrimp mixture. Bake in a 350° oven for 5 to 6 minutes or until cheese begins to melt. Top with tomato mixture. Serve warm.

Toasted Pita Wedges: Split 3 pita bread rounds in half horizontally; cut each circle into 6 wedges. Place the wedges in a single layer on 2 large baking sheets. Bake in a 350° oven for 8 to 10 minutes or until wedges just begin to brown. If desired, seal cooled wedges in a plastic bag and store overnight at room temperature.

Nutrition facts per serving: 91 cal., 4 g total fat (2 g sat. fat), 34 mg chol., 145 mg sodium, 7 g carbo., 0 g fiber, 6 g pro. Daily values: 4% vit. A, 10% vit. C, 8% calcium, 4% iron

toasted almonds with rosemary & cayenne

Sweet, hot, and crunchy. No wonder these herb-coated almonds disappear quickly. Make a bowl—maybe two—especially when you're serving cocktails. Then mix some martinis and kick back to the sounds of some cool jazz.

Start to finish: 15 minutes   Makes 16 servings

Spread almonds in a single layer on a baking sheet. Bake in a 350° oven about 10 minutes or until nuts are lightly toasted and fragrant.

Meanwhile, in a medium saucepan melt butter over medium heat until sizzling. Remove from heat. Stir in rosemary, sugar, salt, and red pepper. Add almonds to butter mixture and toss to coat. Cool slightly before serving. If desired, seal cooled nuts in an airtight container and store for up to 1 month in refrigerator or up to 3 months in freezer.

Nutrition facts per serving: 80 cal., 7 g total fat (1 g sat. fat), 1 mg chol., 37 mg sodium, 3 g carbo., 1 g fiber, 4 g pro. Daily values: 0% vit. A, 0% vit. C, 4% calcium, 5% iron

8	ounces unblanched almonds or pecan halves (about 2 cups)
1½	teaspoons butter
1	tablespoon finely snipped fresh rosemary
1½	teaspoons brown sugar
¼ to ½	teaspoon salt
¼	teaspoon ground red pepper

classic **cocktails**

The cocktail is back! Here's how to make a few of the standbys:

Martini: In a cocktail shaker combine cracked ice, ¼ cup vodka or gin, and a tablespoon of dry vermouth. Shake well to mix. Strain into a chilled cocktail glass. Garnish with a green olive. Makes 1.

Daiquiri: In a cocktail shaker combine cracked ice, 3 tablespoons light rum, 2 tablespoons lime juice, 1 teaspoon powdered sugar, and 1 teaspoon orange liqueur. Shake well to mix; strain into a chilled cocktail glass. Makes 1.

Margarita: In a cocktail shaker combine cracked ice, 3 tablespoons tequila, 2 tablespoons triple sec, and 2 tablespoons lime juice. Shake well to mix. For a salt-rimmed glass, rub the edge of a chilled cocktail glass with a lime wedge; invert into a dish of coarse salt. Strain drink into glass. Makes 1.

asparagus with raspberry-dijon dipping sauce

Why relegate tender asparagus to the side? Here, it stars as a fresh and light starter with a fruity dipping sauce. If you like, prepare the sauce ahead and refrigerate it for up to 4 hours before serving.

Start to finish: 25 minutes   Makes 12 servings

Snap off and discard woody bases from asparagus. If desired, remove tips and strings from sugar snap peas. In a large deep skillet bring 1 inch of salted water to boiling. Add asparagus; reduce heat. Simmer, uncovered, about 4 minutes or until crisp-tender. Using tongs, transfer asparagus to a large bowl of ice water to cool quickly. Add sugar snap peas to simmering water and cook about 2 minutes or until crisp-tender. Drain and transfer to bowl of ice water.

Meanwhile, for dipping sauce, in a blender container or food processor bowl combine vinegar, honey mustard, pepper, and salt. Cover and blend or process until combined. With the blender or processor running, slowly add the oils in a thin, steady stream. Continue blending or processing until mixture is thick.

If desired, line a serving platter with shredded red cabbage. Arrange asparagus and sugar snap peas on top of the cabbage. Serve with dipping sauce. If desired, garnish with raspberries.

Nutrition facts per serving: 96 cal., 9 g total fat (1 g sat. fat), 0 mg chol., 14 mg sodium, 3 g carbo., 1 g fiber, 1 g pro. Daily values: 2% vit. A, 26% vit. C, 1% calcium, 3% iron

1 **pound medium asparagus spears**

8 **ounces sugar snap peas**

3 **tablespoons raspberry vinegar**

1 **tablespoon honey mustard**

¼ **teaspoon freshly ground pepper**

Dash salt

¼ **cup cooking oil**

¼ **cup olive oil**

Shredded red cabbage (optional)

Fresh raspberries (optional)

grilled portobellos
with avocado salsa

Get the party off to a sassy start. Toss portobello mushrooms on the grill and top with salsa for a smoky, rich flavor that will seduce the most timid appetite. For a light entrée, roll up the mushrooms in warm tortillas or serve atop grilled bread.

4 6- to 8-ounce fresh
    portobello mushrooms

3 tablespoons balsamic vinegar

2 tablespoons red wine vinegar

2 tablespoons olive oil

¼ teaspoon crushed red pepper

1 medium avocado, halved,
    seeded, peeled, and chopped

1 medium tomato, chopped

¼ cup sliced green onions

¼ cup crumbled, crisp-cooked bacon

2 tablespoons snipped fresh cilantro

Prep: 20 minutes Cook: 8 minutes   Makes 8 servings

Cut off mushroom stems even with caps; discard stems. In a small bowl combine vinegars, olive oil, and red pepper. Reserve ¼ cup for salsa.

Grill mushroom caps on the rack of an uncovered grill directly over medium heat for 8 to 10 minutes or until tender, turning and brushing once with the remaining vinegar mixture. For salsa, combine reserved vinegar mixture, avocado, tomato, green onions, bacon, and cilantro.

Slice the mushrooms about ½ inch thick. Spoon the salsa over the mushroom slices.

Nutrition facts per serving: 117 cal., 8 g total fat (2 g sat. fat), 2 mg chol., 44 mg sodium, 10 g carbo., 2 g fiber, 3 g pro. Daily values: 4% vit. A, 18% vit. C, 0% calcium, 13% iron

bella portobello!

The big mushroom with the Italian-sounding name isn't Italian at all. The romantic moniker was devised by an American marketer in the 1980s to sell more of these mushrooms, which are the fully mature form of the crimino, a dark-brown variation of the common white button mushroom. The strategy worked. Portobello mushrooms—which can be upwards of 6 inches in diameter—have a rich flavor and dense, meaty texture, making them great candidates for the grill. They're also nice cut into thick slices for topping off a salad. If you can't find portobello mushrooms, you can substitute large, flat white button mushrooms with the stems removed.

vegetable-stuffed tomato bites

A garden of fresh flavors comes together in one bite in these miniature tomato "boats" loaded with sweet corn, crisp jicama, and fresh herbs. Spike the dressing with Gorgonzola cheese for a tangy contrast.

Prep: 20 minutes   Makes 16 to 20 servings

Cut tomatoes in half lengthwise. Scoop out the pulp, leaving ¼-inch-thick shells. Discard pulp. Place the tomato shells, cut sides down, on paper towels. Let stand while preparing filling.

For filling, in a medium bowl combine cheese, green onion, sour cream, mayonnaise or salad dressing, and oregano or basil. Stir in corn and jicama. If desired, cover and refrigerate the tomato shells and filling separately until ready to serve.

To serve, spoon about 1 tablespoon of the corn mixture into each tomato shell. Season to taste with freshly ground pepper.

Nutrition facts per serving: 27 cal., 1 g total fat (1 g sat. fat), 1 mg chol., 41 mg sodium, 3 g carbo., 0 g fiber, 1 g pro. Daily values: 2% vit. A, 10% vit. C, 1% calcium, 1% iron

8 to 10 plum tomatoes
(about 1 pound total)

3 tablespoons crumbled
Gorgonzola or other
blue cheese

2 tablespoons thinly sliced
green onion

2 tablespoons light dairy
sour cream

2 tablespoons light mayonnaise
dressing or salad dressing

1 teaspoon snipped fresh
oregano or basil

¾ cup frozen whole kernel
corn, thawed

¼ cup chopped, peeled jicama

easygoing
entrées

tenderloin steaks with arugula-cornichon relish

Most guests love a good steak, but it's better yet with this caper and fresh-herb relish. Peppery arugula, a built-in salad, offers a pleasant bite. Serve the steaks with mashed potatoes. For dessert, Gingered Shortcake with Spiced Fruit (page 85).

Prep: 20 minutes   Cook: 8 minutes   Makes 4 servings

Trim fat from steaks. Rub both sides of steaks with pepper and salt. In a large skillet heat 1 tablespoon of the olive oil over medium heat. Cook to desired doneness, turning once. (Allow 8 to 11 minutes for medium rare or 12 to 14 minutes for medium doneness.)

Meanwhile, for relish, in a small bowl combine the remaining 2 tablespoons olive oil, the parsley, cornichons or pickles, capers, green onion, and balsamic vinegar. Set aside.

To serve, transfer steaks to a cutting board; cut into thin slices. Arrange the arugula or mixed greens on dinner plates. Top with the steak slices; then spoon the relish over steak and arugula.

Nutrition facts per serving: 273 cal., 18 g total fat (4 g sat. fat), 64 mg chol., 460 mg sodium, 6 g carbo., 1 g fiber, 23 g pro. Daily values: 8% vit. A, 17% vit. C, 4% calcium, 25% iron

4 beef tenderloin steaks (or 2 halved ribeye steaks), cut 1 inch thick (about 1 pound total)

1 tablespoon cracked pepper

½ teaspoon salt

3 tablespoons olive oil

⅓ cup snipped fresh Italian flat-leaf parsley

3 tablespoons finely chopped cornichons or sweet pickles

2 tablespoons capers, drained and coarsely chopped

1 medium green onion, chopped

1 tablespoon balsamic vinegar

3 cups torn arugula and/or torn mixed greens

fajita kabobs

Sizzling platters of fajitas brought tableside may be dramatic, but they're difficult to do for a group. These quick-to-fix kabobs capture the panache of fajitas, but avoid having the skillet under constant surveillance—which means more time with friends.

 1 recipe Pico de Gallo Salsa

½ cup light dairy sour cream

 2 tablespoons snipped fresh cilantro

1¼ pounds beef top sirloin steak, cut 1 inch thick

 3 red and/or green sweet peppers, cut into 1-inch pieces

 1 red onion, cut into wedges

½ cup vinegar and oil salad dressing

½ teaspoon ground cumin

¼ teaspoon crushed red pepper

12 7- to 8-inch flour tortillas

Prep: 40 minutes Grill: 5 minutes Marinate: 2 hours

Makes 6 servings

Prepare Pico de Gallo Salsa. Combine sour cream and cilantro. Cover and refrigerate both mixtures until ready to serve. Trim fat from steak. Cut steak into ¼-inch-thick strips. Place steak strips, sweet peppers, and onion wedges in a plastic bag set in a shallow dish. For marinade, combine salad dressing, cumin, and crushed red pepper. Pour over steak and vegetables; close bag. Marinate in refrigerator for 2 to 24 hours, turning bag occasionally. Wrap tortillas in foil; set aside.

Drain steak and vegetables, discarding marinade. On six 12-inch skewers alternately thread steak, sweet pepper, and onion. Grill kabobs on the rack of an uncovered grill directly over medium heat for 5 to 6 minutes for medium doneness, turning once. Place tortillas to one side of grill while grilling kabobs, turning occasionally. Serve kabobs with tortillas, salsa, and sour cream mixture.

Pico de Gallo Salsa: Combine 2 medium tomatoes, peeled and finely chopped; 2 tablespoons finely chopped onion; 2 tablespoons snipped fresh cilantro or parsley; 1 fresh serrano chili pepper, finely chopped; and dash sugar. Makes about 1 cup.

Nutrition facts per serving: 450 cal., 20 g total fat (6 g sat. fat), 66 mg chol., 367 mg sodium, 38 g carbo., 2 g fiber, 28 g pro. Daily values: 33% vit. A, 120% vit. C, 9% calcium, 34% iron

steak caribbean

Yes, we have grilled bananas—and black beans and rice to complement a coriander-cumin-rubbed steak that conjures up island breezes whatever the weather. One bite and you'll dream you're in a clime where the lime tree grows.

Start to finish: 35 minutes   Makes 4 servings

Trim fat from steaks. Combine garlic, cumin, coriander, salt, and ground red pepper. Reserve ¼ teaspoon spice mixture for rice. Brush both sides of steaks with 1 tablespoon of the lime juice, then rub with remaining spice mixture. Combine remaining 1 tablespoon lime juice, the orange peel, and melted margarine or butter. Brush on both sides of bananas.

Grill steaks on the rack of an uncovered grill directly over medium heat to desired doneness, turning once. (Allow 8 to 12 minutes for medium rare or 12 to 15 minutes for medium doneness.) About halfway through cooking the steaks, add bananas or plaintains directly to grill rack and grill for 5 to 6 minutes or until heated through, turning once.

Meanwhile, cook the rice in lightly salted water according to package directions, except add the reserved spice mixture to cooking liquid. Stir beans and sweet pepper into cooked rice. Heat through and keep warm. Cut each steak in half. Serve steak with rice and bananas.

Nutrition facts per serving: 417 cal., 13 g total fat (5 g sat. fat), 67 mg chol., 214 mg sodium, 46 g carbo., 2 g fiber, 28 g pro. Daily values: 5% vit. A, 24% vit. C, 4% calcium, 35% iron

Note: Fully ripe plantains are still slightly firm but have skin that has turned mostly black. If the plantains are not fully ripe, cook them a few minutes longer than specified in recipe method above.

- **2 beef ribeye steaks, cut 1 inch thick (1 to 1¼ pounds total)**
- **4 cloves garlic, minced**
- **1½ teaspoons ground cumin**
- **1 teaspoon ground coriander**
- **¼ teaspoon salt**
- **⅛ to ¼ teaspoon ground red pepper**
- **2 tablespoons lime juice**
- **1 teaspoon finely shredded orange peel**
- **1 teaspoon margarine or butter, melted**
- **2 large firm bananas or fully ripe plantains*, peeled and cut in half lengthwise and crosswise**
- **⅔ cup uncooked long-grain rice**
- **½ cup cooked or canned black beans, rinsed and drained**
- **2 tablespoons finely chopped red sweet pepper**

beef & vegetable ragout

The earthy, elegant, and traditionally long-simmered French stew called ragout gets an update in taste and reduced preparation time. This version, flavored with port wine and filled with crisp, bright vegetables, can be on the table in 30 minutes.

12 **ounces beef tenderloin, cut into ¾-inch pieces**

1 **tablespoon olive oil or cooking oil**

1½ **cups sliced fresh shiitake or button mushrooms (4 ounces)**

1 **medium onion, chopped**

2 **cloves garlic, minced**

3 **tablespoons all-purpose flour**

½ **teaspoon salt**

¼ **teaspoon pepper**

1 **14½-ounce can beef broth**

¼ **cup port wine or dry sherry**

2 **cups sugar snap peas or one 10-ounce package frozen sugar snap peas, thawed**

1 **cup cherry tomatoes, halved**

Hot cooked wide noodles or bow-tie pasta (optional)

Start to finish: 30 minutes   Makes 4 servings

In a large nonstick skillet cook and stir meat in hot oil for 2 to 3 minutes or until meat is of desired doneness. Remove meat; set aside. In the same skillet cook mushrooms, onion, and garlic until tender.

Stir in flour, salt, and pepper. Add beef broth and wine or sherry. Cook and stir until thickened and bubbly. Stir in sugar snap peas; cook and stir for 2 to 3 minutes more or until peas are tender. Stir in meat and tomatoes; heat through. If desired, serve over noodles.

Nutrition facts per serving: 252 cal., 9 g total fat (3 g sat. fat), 48 mg chol., 647 mg sodium, 17 g carbo., 3 g fiber, 21 g pro. Daily values: 4% vit. A, 74% vit. C, 4% calcium, 32% iron

one-pot meal appeal

There's a reason that casseroles and stews have remained time-honored traditions at the table. The one-pot meal can stand alone, if necessary. All of the elements of the meal are in one place, so there aren't three pots to watch and wash. For casual entertaining, the one-pot meal is ideal. This hearty and flavorful dish can be made ahead and simply reheated while the noodles are cooking (just add the snap peas right before serving so they stay crisp and green). Serve with some crusty bread or corn bread and a salad, if you like, and your company fare is finished.

flank steak with caramelized onions

Scoring the flank steak before cooking and slicing it across the grain makes it tender; cooking the onions slowly in butter makes them sweet and golden. Bundle it all up in tortillas, or serve with Potato-Leek Pancakes (page 78).

24

2 large red onions, halved lengthwise and thinly sliced

2 tablespoons butter or margarine

1 red or green sweet pepper, cut into thin strips

2 teaspoons snipped fresh sage

2 teaspoons snipped fresh oregano

1 1¼- to 1½-pound beef flank steak

1 tablespoon freshly ground or cracked black pepper

Dash salt

4 7- to 8-inch flour tortillas, warmed* (optional)

Start to finish: 30 minutes   Makes 4 servings

In a covered medium skillet cook onions in hot butter or margarine over medium-low heat for 13 to 15 minutes or until onions are tender, stirring occasionally. Add pepper strips, sage, and oregano. Cook, uncovered, over medium-high heat for 4 to 5 minutes or until onions are golden and pepper strips are crisp-tender, stirring constantly.

Meanwhile, trim fat from steak. Score steak on both sides by making shallow cuts at 1-inch intervals in a diamond pattern. Rub both sides with black pepper and salt. Grill steak on the rack of an uncovered grill directly over medium heat to desired doneness, turning once. (Allow 12 to 14 minutes for medium doneness.)

To serve, thinly slice steak diagonally across the grain. If desired, serve steak strips in warm tortillas. Top with the onion mixture.

Nutrition facts per serving: 294 cal., 16 g total fat (8 g sat. fat), 82 mg chol., 186 mg sodium, 9 g carbo., 2 g fiber, 28 g pro. Daily values: 21% vit. A, 60% vit. C, 3% calcium, 22% iron

*Note: To warm tortillas, wrap in foil and place to one side of grill about 10 minutes while grilling steak, turning occasionally. Or, wrap in waxed paper or microwave-safe paper towels and micro-cook on 100% power (high) for 30 to 60 seconds.

rosemary pork chop skillet

Quick-braise hearty pork chops with two kinds of squash, onion, and herbs. This could replace pot roast as the new Sunday dinner favorite. Afterward, brew a pot of coffee and serve it with Apple-Berry "Pie" (page 86).

Start to finish: 35 minutes   Makes 4 servings

Trim fat from chops. Sprinkle chops with salt and pepper. In a 12-inch skillet heat oil over medium-high heat. Add chops and cook about 4 minutes or until browned, turning once. Combine the winter squash, onion, and rosemary; spoon mixture over chops. Pour chicken broth and orange juice over vegetables. Bring to boiling; reduce heat. Simmer, covered, for 10 minutes.

Add the zucchini and sage. Cook, covered, about 5 minutes more or until chops are tender and no longer pink. Using a slotted spoon, transfer chops and vegetables to a serving platter. Cover and keep warm.

Bring the reserved juices in skillet to boiling; reduce heat. Simmer, uncovered, about 5 minutes or until liquid is reduced to about ¼ cup. Spoon over chops and vegetables.

Nutrition facts per serving: 192 cal., 9 g total fat (2 g sat. fat), 48 mg chol., 345 mg sodium, 12 g carbo., 3 g fiber, 16 g pro. Daily values: 43% vit. A, 34% vit. C, 3% calcium, 9% iron

1 pound boneless pork sirloin chops, cut ½ inch thick

½ teaspoon salt

½ teaspoon pepper

1 tablespoon olive oil

2 cups peeled winter squash cut into 1-inch cubes (such as butternut, banana, spaghetti, and/or acorn squash)

1 medium onion, cut into thin wedges

2 teaspoons snipped fresh rosemary

¼ cup chicken broth

¼ cup orange juice

2 medium zucchini, quartered lengthwise and cut into 1-inch pieces

1 teaspoon snipped fresh sage

pork medallions with fennel & pancetta

A little gourmet, a little down-home. Boneless chops and onions experience a bistro-style revival with fresh fennel, Italian bacon, and sage-cream sauce. Round out your meal with steamed green beans and frozen cooked winter squash.

Start to finish: 30 minutes   Makes 4 servings

Trim fat from meat. Cut meat crosswise into 1-inch-thick slices. Place each slice between 2 pieces of plastic wrap. Pound lightly with flat side of a meat mallet to ¼-inch thickness. Remove plastic wrap. Combine flour, salt, and pepper. Coat meat with flour mixture. In a large heavy skillet heat olive oil over high heat. Add meat, half at a time, and cook for 2 to 3 minutes or until meat is slightly pink in center, turning once. (Add more oil if necessary.) Remove from skillet.

In the same skillet cook pancetta over medium-high heat until crisp. Add fennel, onion, and garlic and cook for 3 to 5 minutes or until crisp-tender. Add lemon juice; stir in cream. Bring to boiling; return meat to pan. Cook until meat is heated through and sauce is slightly thickened.

Transfer the meat to a serving platter. Spoon the sauce over the meat.

Nutrition facts per serving: 341 cal., 23 g total fat (10 g sat. fat), 105 mg chol., 175 mg sodium, 12 g carbo., 12 g fiber, 22 g pro. Daily values: 13% vit. A, 19% vit. C, 4% calcium, 10% iron

1	12-ounce pork tenderloin
¼	cup all-purpose flour
	Dash salt
	Dash pepper
2	tablespoons olive oil
2	ounces pancetta (Italian bacon) or bacon, finely chopped
2	fennel bulbs, trimmed and cut crosswise into ¼-inch-thick slices
1	small onion, thinly sliced
2	cloves garlic, minced
2	tablespoons lemon juice
½	cup whipping cream

sausage with polenta & spinach

Peasant food like this rustic bowlful of sausage, polenta, and greens may be everyday eating for alpine-dwelling Italians, but its uncomplicated flavors give it an undeniable specialness. Chocolate Ricotta-Filled Pears (page 93) keep dessert casual, too.

- 12 ounces fresh mild Italian sausage links, bias-sliced ¾ inch thick
- 4 cups water
- ¼ teaspoon salt
- 1 cup quick-cooking polenta
- ¼ cup grated Parmesan cheese
- 1 medium onion, halved lengthwise and thinly sliced
- 4 cloves garlic, minced
- 1 10-ounce package spinach, stems removed and coarsely chopped

  Dash freshly ground pepper

Start to finish: 35 minutes   Makes 4 servings

In a 12-inch skillet cook sausage over medium heat for 8 to 10 minutes or until no longer pink, stirring frequently. Meanwhile, in a medium saucepan bring water and salt to boiling. Slowly add polenta, stirring constantly until mixture is smooth. Reduce heat; cook and stir for 2 minutes. Cover loosely and cook about 3 minutes more or until thickened, stirring occasionally. Stir in cheese; cover and keep warm.

Remove sausage, reserving 1 tablespoon drippings in skillet. Cover sausage and keep warm. Add onion and garlic to skillet; cook and stir about 4 minutes or until onion is tender. Stir in spinach; cover and cook for 1 to 2 minutes or until spinach is wilted. Sprinkle with pepper.

To serve, spoon the polenta onto dinner plates. Spoon the spinach mixture over polenta. Top with the sausage.

Nutrition facts per serving: 506 cal., 19 g total fat (7 g sat. fat), 54 mg chol., 887 mg sodium, 60 g carbo., 9 g fiber, 23 g pro. Daily values: 48% vit. A, 37% vit. C, 16% calcium, 25% iron

lamb chops with sweet potato chutney

Petite lamb chops make simple but pretty company fare—especially when they're crowned with a richly colored and flavor-packed homemade chutney. Try Corn Cakes with Fresh Corn & Chives (page 76) as an accompaniment.

Prep: 20 minutes   Cook: 10 minutes   Makes 4 servings

Trim fat from chops. In a small bowl combine shallots and red pepper. Reserve 2 tablespoons shallot mixture for chutney. Rub both sides of chops with the remaining shallot mixture. Place chops on the unheated rack of a broiler pan. Set aside.

For chutney, in a medium saucepan combine reserved shallot mixture, the brown sugar, vinegar, dried cranberries or currants, and gingerroot. Stir in sweet potato. Bring to boiling; reduce heat. Simmer, covered, for 10 minutes, stirring occasionally.

Meanwhile, broil chops 3 to 4 inches from the heat to desired doneness, turning once. (Allow 7 to 11 minutes for medium doneness.) Serve the chops with the chutney.

Nutrition facts per serving: 317 cal., 11 g total fat (4 g sat. fat), 97 mg chol., 83 mg sodium, 24 g carbo., 1 g fiber, 30 g pro. Daily values: 81% vit. A, 13% vit. C, 3% calcium, 22% iron

- 8 lamb rib or loin chops, cut 1 inch thick
- $\frac{1}{3}$ cup finely chopped shallots
- $\frac{1}{4}$ teaspoon crushed red pepper
- $\frac{1}{4}$ cup packed brown sugar
- $\frac{1}{4}$ cup vinegar
- 2 tablespoons dried cranberries or currants
- $\frac{1}{2}$ teaspoon grated gingerroot
- 1 medium sweet potato, peeled and cubed

grilled lamburger roll-ups

Here's perfect alfresco food for friends! Spinach, seasoned lamb, and hummus are rolled up in soft cracker bread and cut into eye-catching spirals. For dessert, offer Red Wine-Marinated Peaches (page 91) with coffee or mint tea.

1 **beaten egg**

3 **tablespoons fine dry bread crumbs**

2 **tablespoons snipped fresh oregano**

2 **cloves garlic, minced**

¾ **teaspoon salt**

½ **teaspoon freshly ground pepper**

1 **pound lean ground lamb**

2 **14- to 15-inch soft cracker bread rounds or four 7- to 8-inch flour tortillas**

⅓ **cup prepared hummus (garbanzo bean spread)**

4 **cups torn spinach or red-tipped leaf lettuce**

¼ **cup crumbled feta cheese**

3 **tablespoons sliced pitted kalamata or ripe olives**

Start to finish: 30 minutes   Makes 4 servings

In a large bowl combine egg, bread crumbs, oregano, garlic, salt, pepper, and 1 tablespoon water. Add lamb; mix well. Form into eight 4-inch-long logs.

Grill lamb on the rack of an uncovered grill directly over medium heat for 14 to 18 minutes or until lamb is no longer pink, turning once. (Or, place in shallow baking pan. Bake in a 400° oven for 12 to 14 minutes.)

Meanwhile, spread the cracker bread or tortillas with hummus. Sprinkle with spinach or lettuce, feta cheese, and olives. If using cracker bread, place 4 lamb pieces, end to end, near an edge of each piece. Roll up, beginning with edge closest to lamb. Slice each roll-up diagonally in fourths. (If using tortillas, place 2 lamb pieces, end to end, on each tortilla. Roll up. Slice each roll-up diagonally in half.)

Nutrition facts per serving: 625 cal., 26 g total fat (9 g sat. fat), 135 mg chol., 1,225 mg sodium, 64 g carbo., 2 g fiber, 34 g pro. Daily values: 41% vit. A, 30% vit. C, 11% calcium, 38% iron

cardamom-grilled chicken with pineapple relish

Indian cuisine influences this refreshingly different chicken dish. If you have an Indian grocery store nearby, the crisp pepper-and-lentil crackers called pappadam served with Cucumber Raita (page 75) make terrific appetizers.

4 **medium skinless, boneless chicken breast halves (about 1 pound total)**

¾ **teaspoon ground cardamom**

½ **to 1 teaspoon coarsely ground black pepper**

½ **teaspoon salt**

2 **teaspoons olive oil**

½ **of a medium pineapple, peeled, cored, and chopped (1⅔ cups)**

½ **of a medium red sweet pepper, finely chopped**

2 **tablespoons snipped fresh cilantro or parsley**

2 **tablespoons lime juice**

1 **green onion, thinly sliced**

1 **fresh jalapeño pepper, seeded and finely chopped**

Prep: 20 minutes Grill: 12 minutes   Makes 4 servings

Rinse chicken; pat dry. In a small bowl combine ½ teaspoon of the cardamom, the black pepper, and salt. Rub both sides of chicken with olive oil; then sprinkle with spice mixture.

Grill chicken on the rack of an uncovered grill directly over medium heat for 12 to 15 minutes or until chicken is tender and no longer pink, turning once.

For relish, in a medium bowl combine pineapple, sweet pepper, cilantro or parsley, lime juice, green onion, jalapeño pepper, and the remaining ¼ teaspoon cardamom. Serve chicken with relish.

Nutrition facts per serving: 180 cal., 6 g total fat (1 g sat. fat), 59 mg chol., 322 mg sodium, 10 g carbo., 1 g fiber, 22 g pro. Daily values: 8% vit. A, 57% vit. C, 1% calcium, 8% iron

spice is nice

Cardamom is a pungent and aromatic spice with a flowery sweetness that's a bit like ginger but much more subtle. Whole cardamom pods, whole seeds, and ground cardamom seeds are all available. You'll find ground cardamom at your grocery store; if you prefer to grind your own, the pods are available at Asian and Scandinavian markets and health food stores.

sautéed chicken breasts with tomatillo salsa

Although tomatillos look like tiny green tomatoes, their acidic flavor hints of lemon and apple. They're commonly used in Southwest-inspired cooking. Tomatillo salsa puts zest in these chili-cornmeal-breaded chicken breasts.

33

Start to finish: 25 minutes   Makes 4 servings

Rinse chicken; pat dry. In a plastic bag combine cornmeal, flour, 3 teaspoons (1 tablespoon) of the chili powder, the salt, and pepper. Add chicken, 2 pieces at a time, and shake to coat.

In a large skillet heat cooking oil over medium heat. Add chicken and cook for 8 to 10 minutes or until chicken is tender and no longer pink, turning once.

Meanwhile, for tomatillo salsa, drain, rinse, and coarsely chop tomatillos (you should have about 1 cup). In a small bowl combine tomatillos, cilantro, onion, lime juice, jalapeño pepper, and the remaining 1 teaspoon chili powder. Serve the chicken with salsa.

Nutrition facts per serving: 240 cal., 10 g total fat (2 g sat. fat), 59 mg chol., 755 mg sodium, 13 g carbo., 1 g fiber, 23 g pro. Daily values: 10% vit. A, 17% vit. C, 1% calcium, 10% iron

4 medium skinless, boneless chicken breast halves (about 1 pound total)

2 tablespoons yellow cornmeal

2 tablespoons all-purpose flour

4 teaspoons chili powder

½ teaspoon salt

¼ teaspoon pepper

2 tablespoons cooking oil

1 13-ounce can tomatillos

3 tablespoons snipped fresh cilantro

3 tablespoons finely chopped onion

2 tablespoons lime juice

1 fresh jalapeño pepper, seeded and finely chopped

sautéed chicken with brandied fruit & almonds

Ground red pepper heats, just enough, these scaloppine-style chicken breasts dressed with a sweet, aromatic nectarine sauce. Add a tossed spinach salad on the side.

Start to finish: 30 minutes   Makes 4 servings

Rinse chicken; pat dry. Place each chicken piece between 2 pieces of plastic wrap. Pound lightly with the flat side of a meat mallet to ¼-inch thickness. Remove plastic wrap. Combine flour, salt, and red pepper. Coat chicken pieces with flour mixture.

In a large skillet heat olive oil and butter or margarine over medium heat. Add chicken and cook for 6 to 8 minutes or until chicken is tender and no longer pink, turning once. Remove skillet from heat. Transfer chicken to a serving platter; cover and keep warm. Add nectarines, brandy, lemon juice, and 2 tablespoons water to the skillet. Return to heat and cook for 1 minute, stirring gently.

Serve the fruit mixture over chicken. Sprinkle with almonds. If desired, garnish with oregano.

Nutrition facts per serving: 303 cal., 12 g total fat (3 g sat. fat), 67 mg chol., 217 mg sodium, 19 g carbo., 2 g fiber, 24 g pro. Daily values: 10% vit. A, 12% vit. C, 2% calcium, 9% iron

Note: Fresh plums, peaches, or pears can be substituted for the nectarines.

4 medium skinless, boneless chicken breast halves (about 1 pound total)

¼ cup all-purpose flour

¼ teaspoon salt

⅛ teaspoon ground red pepper

1 tablespoon olive oil

1 tablespoon butter or margarine

3 medium nectarines, pitted and cut into thin wedges*

3 tablespoons brandy

1 tablespoon lemon juice

2 tablespoons sliced almonds, toasted

Fresh oregano sprigs (optional)

chicken souvlaki

What the kabob is to the Middle East, skewered souvlaki is to Greece. Rosemary and thyme, which cover the hillsides of the Greek Islands, add authentic flavor to the marinade. Use a sprig of rosemary to brush the marinade on the assorted vegetables.

1 pound skinless, boneless chicken thighs or breasts

⅓ cup vinegar and oil salad dressing

1 teaspoon finely shredded lemon peel

1 tablespoon lemon juice

1 teaspoon snipped fresh rosemary or ¼ teaspoon dried rosemary, crushed

1 teaspoon snipped fresh thyme or ¼ teaspoon dried thyme, crushed

2 small green peppers, cut into 1-inch pieces

1 medium onion, cut into 8 wedges

3 cups hot cooked rice

Prep: 25 minutes Marinate: 3 hours Broil: 10 minutes
Makes 4 servings

Rinse chicken; pat dry. Cut chicken into 1-inch pieces. Place chicken in a plastic bag set in a shallow bowl. For marinade, combine salad dressing, lemon peel, lemon juice, rosemary, and thyme. Pour over chicken; close bag. Marinate in refrigerator for 3 to 24 hours, turning bag occasionally.

Drain chicken, reserving marinade. On eight 8-inch skewers* alternately thread chicken, green peppers, and onion. Brush peppers and onion with reserved marinade. Place kabobs on the unheated rack of a broiler pan. Broil 3 to 4 inches from heat for 10 to 12 minutes or until chicken is tender and no longer pink, turning once. (Or, grill on the rack of an uncovered grill directly over medium heat for 10 to 12 minutes, turning once.) Serve with rice.

Nutrition facts per serving: 392 cal., 17 g total fat (3 g sat. fat), 54 mg chol., 337 mg sodium, 41 g carbo., 1 g fiber, 20 g pro. Daily values: 4% vit. A, 90% vit. C, 2% calcium, 17% iron

Note: If you like, use rosemary sticks for skewers. Be sure to soak the sticks in water for 1 hour before making the kabobs.

plum-sauced chicken salad

Plum jam and fresh plums bathe these lemon-peppered chicken breasts in rich colors. A hint of fresh ginger enhances the sauce, too. Just add some rolls from your favorite bakery, and dinner is complete.

Start to finish: 30 minutes   Makes 4 servings

Rinse chicken; pat day. Sprinkle both sides of chicken with lemon-pepper seasoning. In a large skillet melt margarine or butter over medium heat. Add chicken and cook for 8 to 10 minutes or until chicken is tender and no longer pink, turning once. Remove from the skillet; cover and keep warm.

Add gingerroot to drippings in skillet and cook and stir for 30 seconds. Carefully stir in plum jam and salad dressing. Cook until jam is melted, stirring occasionally. Stir in fruit and heat just until warm.

To serve, arrange the greens on dinner plates. Top with the chicken and fruit mixture.

Nutrition facts per serving: 424 cal., 16 g total fat (3 g sat. fat), 59 mg chol., 692 mg sodium, 46 g carbo., 3 g fiber, 23 g pro. Daily values: 22% vit. A, 60% vit. C, 4% calcium, 12% iron

4 medium skinless, boneless
    chicken breast halves
    (about 1 pound total)

1 teaspoon lemon-pepper seasoning

2 tablespoons margarine or butter

1 teaspoon grated gingerroot

½ cup plum jam

¼ cup red wine vinegar and
    oil salad dressing

3 cups fresh fruit (such as plum
    or apricot wedges, quartered
    pineapple slices, sliced kiwifruit,
    cut-up peeled mango or papaya,
    sliced nectarines or peeled
    peaches, and/or halved grapes)

4 cups torn mixed greens

braised chicken thighs with peppers & olives

Saffron colors this Spanish dish a sunny yellow. This prized spice is actually the dried stigmas of the crocus flower, which must be handpicked. Note to food-trivia lovers: About 250,000 stigmas make a pound. The pungent taste is well worth the high price.

12 skinless, boneless chicken thighs
    (2 to 2½ pounds total)

2 tablespoons olive oil

1 large onion, chopped

1 medium red sweet pepper,
   cut into thin strips

3 cloves garlic, minced

1 cup uncooked long-grain rice

¼ teaspoon thread saffron, crushed,
   or ⅛ teaspoon ground saffron

½ cup pimiento-stuffed green
   olives, halved

½ cup dry white wine, dry vermouth,
   or chicken broth

   Lemon wedges

Start to finish: 45 minutes   Makes 6 servings

Rinse chicken; pat dry. Sprinkle chicken with salt and pepper. In a 12-inch skillet heat olive oil over medium-high heat. Add chicken and cook about 10 minutes or until browned, turning once. Remove chicken, reserving 1 tablespoon drippings in skillet.

Add onion, sweet pepper, and garlic to skillet; cook and stir for 4 to 5 minutes or until vegetables are tender. Stir in rice and saffron; add olives, wine, vermouth or chicken broth, and 1½ cups water. Bring to boiling. Return chicken to skillet; reduce heat. Simmer, covered, about 25 minutes or until chicken is no longer pink and rice is tender. Serve with lemon wedges.

Nutrition facts per serving: 328 cal., 11 g total fat (3 g sat. fat), 73 mg chol., 338 mg sodium, 28 g carbo., 1 g fiber, 24 g pro. Daily values: 11% vit. A, 36% vit. C, 3% calcium, 18% iron

posole verde

Buy a salsa verde (green sauce) containing mostly jalapeños if you like your soup on the fiery side—or one made mostly from tomatillos if you like it kinder and gentler. Serve it with warm tortillas or corn bread and a dollop of sour cream on top.

1 medium zucchini

2 fresh ears of corn or 1 cup frozen whole kernel corn

1 medium onion, chopped

1 tablespoon cooking oil

2 14½-ounce cans reduced-sodium chicken broth

½ cup green salsa

2 cups cooked turkey cut into bite-size strips

Assorted toppings (such as sour cream, sliced radishes, sliced avocado, sliced green onion, and/or chopped jalapeño pepper) (optional)

Start to finish: 25 minutes   Makes 4 to 6 servings

Quarter zucchini lengthwise and cut into ½-inch pieces. If using fresh corn, cut kernels from cobs. Set aside. In a large saucepan cook onion in hot oil until tender. Stir in broth and salsa.

Bring to boiling. Stir in zucchini, corn, and turkey. Return to boiling; reduce heat. Simmer, uncovered, about 5 minutes or until vegetables are just tender. Serve in bowls. If desired, pass toppings.

Nutrition facts per serving: 266 cal., 12 g total fat (3 g sat. fat), 71 mg chol., 772 mg sodium, 15 g carbo., 3 g fiber, 24 g pro. Daily values: 8% vit. A, 18% vit. C, 2% calcium, 12% iron

food fashion

When it comes to garnishing fresh and simple food, there is only one rule: Keep it simple. It might be as fuss-free as a sprig of fresh herb or a sprinkle of freshly ground pepper, ground spice, or chopped nuts. Consider pooling a sauce under the food, as well as spooning some on top. Cut food into interesting shapes: bias-slice carrots, thinly slice cucumbers and peppers, shred radishes, and so on.

moroccan turkey burgers

What gives thoroughly American burgers served on sesame-seed buns Moroccan flair? Raisins, almonds, aromatic coriander and cumin, and a fresh mint-infused sauce. Serve with sweet-potato chips (try gourmet food or health-food stores) and iced mint tea.

Prep: 20 minutes Broil: 10 minutes   Makes 4 servings

In a small bowl combine sour cream and mint. Cover and refrigerate until ready to serve. In a medium bowl combine turkey or chicken, raisins, almonds, salt, pepper, coriander, and cumin. Mix well. Form into four ¾-inch-thick patties.

Place burgers on the unheated rack of a broiler pan. Broil 4 to 5 inches from heat for 10 to 12 minutes or until no longer pink, turning once. Serve on sesame buns and top with sour cream mixture.

Nutrition facts per serving: 336 cal., 16 g total fat (5 g sat. fat), 49 mg chol., 396 mg sodium, 28 g carbo., 1 g fiber, 20 g pro. Daily values: 3% vit. A, 1% vit. C, 6% calcium, 18% iron

- ¼ cup regular or light dairy sour cream
- 1 teaspoon snipped fresh mint
- 1 pound ground raw turkey or chicken
- 3 tablespoons chopped raisins
- 2 tablespoons chopped slivered almonds
- ¼ teaspoon salt
- ¼ teaspoon coarsely ground pepper
- ¼ teaspoon ground coriander
- ¼ teaspoon ground cumin
- 4 sesame hamburger buns, split and toasted

ground rules

Ground beef has long been around as a convenient, quick-cooking food, so it's only logical that poultry-lovers would popularize ground turkey and chicken. Ground turkey and chicken can be light and healthful alternatives to ground beef in many dishes—if you make sure they're prepared after the skin and fat have been removed. Most of the ground turkey and chicken you find in your grocery store meat department is ground with the skin on. To assure your ground poultry is low fat, look for labels that say something like "diet lean" or "98% lean." That usually means it's made from skinless breast meat only. Better yet, have your butcher grind specific pieces of meat for you. Then you know it's fresh and low fat.

pan-seared salmon with stir-fried vegetables

Salmon gets Pan-Asian treatment in this dish with a trio of matchstick-sliced vegetables and a homemade teriyaki sauce fired up with five-spice powder—a mix of star anise, ginger, cinnamon, cloves, and Szechwan peppercorns.

Start to finish: 35 minutes   Makes 4 servings

Rinse fish; pat dry. Cut fish into 4 serving-size pieces. Set aside. In a small bowl combine 1 tablespoon of the sherry, 1 tablespoon of the soy sauce, the sesame oil, cornstarch, ¼ teaspoon of the five-spice powder, the sugar, and 3 tablespoons water. Set aside.

In another small bowl combine the remaining 1 tablespoon sherry, 1 tablespoon soy sauce, ¼ teaspoon five-spice powder, and 1 tablespoon water. Brush over the salmon pieces. In a large skillet heat oil over medium heat. Add salmon; cook for 6 to 9 minutes or until fish flakes easily with a fork, turning once. Remove; cover and keep warm.

In the same skillet stir-fry carrots, celery, garlic, and gingerroot for 3 minutes. Add green onions and stir-fry for 1 minute more or until vegetables are crisp-tender. Push vegetables from center of skillet. Stir cornstarch mixture and add to center of skillet. Cook and stir until thickened and bubbly. Cook and stir for 2 minutes more. Stir vegetables into sauce to coat.

To serve, spoon the vegetable mixture onto dinner plates. Top with the salmon. If desired, season to taste with salt and pepper.

Nutrition facts per serving: 274 cal., 15 g total fat (3 g sat. fat), 25 mg chol., 677 mg sodium, 11 g carbo., 3 g fiber, 22 g pro. Daily values: 127% vit. A, 13% vit. C, 5% calcium, 13% iron

- 1¼ **pounds skinless fresh salmon fillets, ¾ inch thick**
- 2 **tablespoons dry sherry**
- 2 **tablespoons soy sauce**
- 1 **tablespoon toasted sesame oil**
- 1 **teaspoon cornstarch**
- ½ **teaspoon five-spice powder**
- ¼ **teaspoon sugar**
- 2 **tablespoons cooking oil**
- 3 **medium carrots, cut into thin 2-inch-long strips**
- 3 **stalks celery, thinly sliced**
- 2 **cloves garlic, minced**
- 2 **teaspoons grated gingerroot**
- 6 **medium green onions, cut into 1-inch lengths**

seared tuna with grapefruit-orange relish

Tuna steak stays moist and flavorful when cooked as quickly as possible. Pan-searing over high heat is ideal—it seals the juices on the inside and gives the outside an irresistible caramel-colored crust.

44

2 teaspoons sherry vinegar
  or white wine vinegar

2 teaspoons soy sauce

½ teaspoon grated gingerroot

1 tablespoon olive oil

1 medium grapefruit, peeled
  and sectioned

1 medium orange, peeled
  and sectioned

2 tablespoons finely
  chopped red onion

2 tablespoons snipped fresh cilantro

4 4-ounce fresh tuna steaks,
  cut ¾ inch thick

2 teaspoons olive oil

  Fresh cilantro sprigs (optional)

Prep: 20 minutes Cook: 6 minutes   Makes 4 servings

For citrus relish, in a small bowl combine vinegar, soy sauce, and gingerroot. Whisk in the 1 tablespoon olive oil. Cut grapefruit sections into thirds and orange sections in half. Stir fruit pieces, red onion, and the 2 tablespoons cilantro into vinegar mixture. Set aside.

Rinse fish; pat dry. In a large skillet heat the 2 teaspoons olive oil over medium-high heat. Add fish and cook for 6 to 9 minutes or until fish flakes easily with a fork, turning once. Sprinkle with salt and pepper. Serve the fish with citrus relish. If desired, garnish with cilantro sprigs.

Nutrition facts per serving: 256 cal., 12 g total fat (2 g sat. fat), 47 mg chol., 287 mg sodium, 7 g carbo., 1 g fiber, 29 g pro. Daily values: 74% vit. A, 51% vit. C, 2% calcium, 9% iron

fish market

When shopping for fresh fish, choose only fish that has a mild smell, not a strong odor. If you're buying a whole fish, look for eyes that are clear and bright, not sunken. Select fish with bright red or pink gills and skin that is shiny and elastic with the scales tightly in place. If you're buying fresh fillets and steaks, choose ones that appear moist and recently cut. Fresh fish is very perishable, so it's best to cook it the same day you buy it. If that's not possible, store fish in the coldest part of the refrigerator (usually the bottom shelf) for up to 2 days, or freeze it. Be sure that it is properly wrapped in moisture-and-vaporproof material.

greek-style swordfish with lemon orzo

Tsatsiki, a garlic- and dill-infused cucumber-yogurt sauce, tops this grilled swordfish. Just one taste will transport you to a romantic taverna table in the Plaka, the old town district in Athens.

4	4-ounce fresh or frozen swordfish steaks, cut 1 inch thick
½	of a small cucumber, peeled, halved lengthwise, and seeded
½	cup plain fat-free yogurt
1	clove garlic, minced
1	tablespoon walnut pieces
1	teaspoon olive oil
1½	teaspoons snipped fresh dill
1	tablespoon olive oil
½	teaspoon salt
¼	teaspoon freshly ground black pepper
1	cup dried orzo pasta (rosamarina)
¼	cup crumbled feta cheese (1 ounce)
1	tablespoon olive oil
1	tablespoon lemon juice

Prep: 20 minutes Grill: 8 minutes   Makes 4 servings

Thaw fish, if frozen. For sauce, coarsely chop half of the cucumber; finely chop remaining cucumber. In a food processor bowl or blender container combine coarsely chopped cucumber, 2 tablespoons of the yogurt, the garlic, walnuts, and the 1 teaspoon oil. Cover and process or blend until smooth. Transfer to a small bowl; stir in finely chopped cucumber, remaining yogurt, and dill.

Rinse fish; pat dry. Brush with 1 tablespoon oil; sprinkle with salt and pepper. Grill fish on the greased rack of an uncovered grill directly over medium heat for 8 to 12 minutes or until fish flakes easily with a fork, turning once. (Or, broil on the greased unheated rack of a broiler pan 4 inches from heat for 8 to 12 minutes, turning once.)

Meanwhile, cook pasta according to package directions. Drain. Return pasta to hot pan. Add feta cheese, 1 tablespoon oil, and lemon juice; toss to coat. Season with salt and pepper. Spoon sauce on top of fish. Serve with pasta.

Nutrition facts per serving: 379 cal., 17 g total fat (5 g sat. fat), 59 mg chol., 637 mg sodium, 24 g carbo., 0 g fiber, 30 g pro. Daily values: 5% vit. A, 7% vit. C, 12% calcium, 15% iron

seafood confetti cakes with lemon sauce

These seafood cakes measure up to New England's finest. Colorful sweet peppers and fresh Italian parsley brighten a mix of shrimp and crab. Get in a seafood-shack mood: Cover the table with brown paper and serve frosty mugs of beer.

47

Prep: 18 minutes Cook: 12 minutes   Makes 4 servings

In a medium bowl combine egg, mayonnaise or salad dressing, bread crumbs, peppers, and parsley. Add crabmeat and shrimp; mix well. Form into eight 1-inch-thick patties. Place flour in a shallow dish. Coat both sides of seafood cakes with flour.

In a large nonstick skillet heat oil over medium heat. Add seafood cakes, half at a time, and cook about 6 minutes or until golden brown, turning once. Drain on paper towels. (Keep first batch warm in a 300° oven while frying remaining cakes.) Serve with Lemon Sauce.

Lemon Sauce: In a small bowl combine ¼ cup light mayonnaise dressing or salad dressing, 2 tablespoons light dairy sour cream, 1 tablespoon snipped fresh Italian flat-leaf parsley, 1 teaspoon finely shredded lemon peel, and 1 teaspoon lemon juice.

Nutrition facts per serving: 344 cal., 20 g total fat (4 g sat. fat), 198 mg chol., 549 mg sodium, 14 g carbo., 0 g fiber, 25 g pro. Daily values: 10% vit. A, 29% vit. C, 8% calcium, 18% iron

1 **beaten egg**

¼ **cup light mayonnaise dressing or salad dressing**

¼ **cup fine dry bread crumbs**

2 **tablespoons finely chopped red sweet pepper**

2 **tablespoons finely chopped yellow sweet pepper**

1 **tablespoon snipped fresh Italian flat-leaf parsley**

8 **ounces cooked crabmeat, chopped**

8 **ounces frozen shrimp, thawed and finely chopped**

¼ **cup all-purpose flour**

2 **tablespoons cooking oil**

1 **recipe Lemon Sauce**

thai shrimp & fresh vegetable rice

One great marinade makes an unforgettable meal. If you have time, let the shrimp soak up the lime, soy sauce, and ginger flavors for up to two hours before it's stirred into rice studded with asparagus, sweet red pepper, and peanuts.

Start to finish: 30 minutes   Makes 4 servings

Thaw shrimp, if frozen. Rinse shrimp; pat dry. Place shrimp in medium bowl. For marinade, combine lime juice, soy sauce, jalapeño pepper, gingerroot, and garlic. Pour over shrimp; toss to coat. Marinate at room temperature for 15 minutes or cover and marinate in refrigerator for up to 2 hours, stirring occasionally. Drain shrimp well, reserving marinade.

Heat oil in a wok or large skillet over medium-high heat. (Add more oil if necessary during cooking.) Stir-fry shrimp in hot oil for 2 to 3 minutes or until shrimp turn pink. Remove from wok; cover and keep warm. Add asparagus and pepper strips to wok; stir-fry for 2 to 3 minutes or until crisp-tender. Add reserved marinade to wok and bring just to boiling. Stir in cooked rice and peanuts.

To serve, transfer rice mixture to individual bowls or dinner plates. Spoon shrimp on top.

Nutrition facts per serving: 331 cal., 9 g total fat (1 g sat. fat), 131 mg chol., 571 mg sodium, 41 g carbo., 2 g fiber, 22 g pro. Daily values: 20% vit. A, 81% vit. C, 5% calcium, 28% iron

12 ounces fresh or frozen peeled and deveined medium shrimp

2 tablespoons lime juice

4 teaspoons soy sauce

1 fresh jalapeño pepper, seeded and finely chopped

1 teaspoon grated gingerroot

1 clove garlic, minced

1 tablespoon cooking oil

1 pound asparagus spears, bias-sliced 1 inch thick

1 small red sweet pepper, cut into thin bite-size strips

3 cups hot cooked rice

¼ cup chopped peanuts

in the mood
for noodles

wild mushroom ravioli with sage butter

Here's a great tip for making quick work of homemade ravioli: Use wonton wrappers. Northern Italian cuisine rules this recipe, from the woodsiness of the porcini mushroom filling to the sage-butter and Parmesan toppings.

Start to finish: 35 minutes   Makes 4 main-dish servings

Soak dried mushrooms in 1 cup boiling water about 15 minutes or until soft. Drain; squeeze and finely chop mushrooms. Meanwhile, in a large skillet cook fresh mushrooms in hot olive oil over medium-high heat about 5 minutes or until liquid evaporates. Add porcini mushrooms, parsley, and garlic; cook for 1 minute more. Sprinkle with salt and pepper. In a medium bowl combine mushroom mixture, ricotta, and egg yolk. If desired, cover and refrigerate until needed.

For each ravioli, spoon 1 tablespoon mushroom mixture onto a wonton wrapper. Brush egg white around edges and top with another wrapper; press to seal.

In 2 large saucepans bring large amounts of water to boiling. Add half of the ravioli to each pan; cook for 3 to 5 minutes or until tender. Meanwhile, combine melted butter and the 2 teaspoons sage. With a large slotted spoon, transfer cooked ravioli to soup plates. Drizzle with butter mixture and sprinkle with Parmesan cheese. If desired, garnish with sage sprigs.

Nutrition facts per serving: 537 cal., 21 g total fat (9 g sat. fat), 100 mg chol., 935 mg sodium, 67 g carbo., 2 g fiber, 21 g pro. Daily values: 21% vit. A, 9% vit. C, 23% calcium, 33% iron

1	ounce dried porcini mushrooms
8	ounces fresh mushrooms, finely chopped (1⅔ cups)
2	tablespoons olive oil or cooking oil
2	tablespoons snipped fresh Italian flat-leaf parsley
2	cloves garlic, minced
¼	teaspoon salt
⅛	teaspoon pepper
¾	cup ricotta cheese
1	egg yolk
48	wonton wrappers (about 12 ounces)
1	slightly beaten egg white
2	tablespoons butter, melted
2	teaspoons snipped fresh sage
¼	cup shaved Parmesan cheese
	Fresh sage sprigs (optional)

rigatoni & vegetables alfredo

The classic Provençal relish called ratatouille—a mélange of eggplant, tomatoes, onion, zucchini, garlic, and fresh herb—inspires this creamy pasta dish.

6 ounces dried rigatoni or mostaccioli pasta

1 small eggplant, cut into ¾-inch pieces (about 12 ounces)

1 medium onion, chopped

2 tablespoons cooking oil

1 medium zucchini or yellow summer squash, quartered lengthwise and cut into ½-inch pieces

1 10-ounce container refrigerated light alfredo sauce

½ teaspoon garlic salt

2 medium tomatoes, seeded and chopped

½ cup shredded Asiago cheese (2 ounces)

1 tablespoon snipped fresh basil

Start to finish: 25 minutes   Makes 6 main-dish servings

Cook pasta according to package directions. Drain. Meanwhile, in a 12-inch skillet cook eggplant and onion in hot oil for 3 minutes. Add zucchini or summer squash and cook for 2 to 3 minutes more or until zucchini or summer squash is crisp-tender.

Stir in alfredo sauce, garlic salt, and cooked pasta; heat through. Transfer to a serving dish. Top with chopped tomatoes, Asiago cheese, and basil.

Nutrition facts per serving: 332 cal., 15 g total fat (5 g sat. fat), 27 mg chol., 695 mg sodium, 40 g carbo., 3 g fiber, 12 g pro. Daily values: 9% vit. A, 16% vit. C, 16% calcium, 10% iron

fresh is best

Fresh herbs impart an undeniably superior flavor and aroma to foods—so try to use them whenever possible. An easy way to have fresh herbs at your fingertips is to grow them in your garden or in pots on your windowsill. Most grocery stores carry them, too. When purchasing fresh herbs, look for perky leaves with no brown spots. Fresh herbs are highly perishable, so buy them as you need them. For short-term storage, immerse freshly cut stems in water about 2 inches deep. Cover the leaves loosely with a plastic bag or plastic wrap and chill for several days. When fresh herbs aren't available, substitute dried. A guideline for substituting is to use a third less of dried herb (if a recipe calls for 1 tablespoon fresh herb, use 1 teaspoon dried herb).

spaghetti with scallops, spinach, & lemon

The favorite flavors of seafood and lemon come together in this scallop-studded spaghetti dish. The absence of cheese in the pasta makes a cheese platter a perfect prelude, or try Tomato & Olive Crostini (page 9) paired with fresh mozzarella.

53

Start to finish: 25 minutes   Makes 4 main-dish servings

Cook pasta in lightly salted water according to package directions. Drain. Return pasta to hot pan.

Meanwhile, rinse scallops; pat dry. Halve any large scallops. In a large skillet melt butter over medium heat. Add scallops, garlic, lemon peel, and red pepper and cook for 3 to 4 minutes or until scallops turn opaque. Add lemon juice; toss to coat. Add scallop mixture, spinach, and carrot to cooked pasta; toss gently to combine.

Nutrition facts per serving: 370 cal., 8 g total fat (4 g sat. fat), 49 mg chol., 262 mg sodium, 52 g carbo., 2 g fiber, 24 g pro. Daily values: 102% vit. A, 24% vit. C, 10% calcium, 34% iron

8 **ounces dried spaghetti**

1 **pound fresh sea scallops**

2 **tablespoons butter**

3 **cloves garlic, minced**

½ **teaspoon finely shredded lemon peel**

¼ **teaspoon crushed red pepper**

2 **tablespoons lemon juice**

2 **cups shredded spinach**

1 **cup coarsely shredded carrot**

scallop sense

Sea scallops and bay scallops are the two most widely available varieties of this type of shellfish, with sea scallops being the larger and less expensive of the two. Both varieties are known for their rich, slightly sweet flavor, especially the smaller bay scallops. Fresh scallops should be firm, sweet smelling, and free of excess cloudy liquid. Chill shucked scallops covered with their own liquid in a tightly closed container for up to 2 days.

pasta rosa-verde

This red, white, and green dish on the table will make any flag-waving Italian feel patriotic (not to mention famished)! Fresh tomatoes are quick-cooked with peppery arugula and topped with tangy Gorgonzola cheese.

8 ounces dried ziti or
   mostaccioli pasta

1 medium onion, thinly sliced

2 cloves garlic, minced

1 tablespoon olive oil

4 to 6 medium tomatoes, seeded
   and coarsely chopped (3 cups)

1 teaspoon salt

½ teaspoon freshly ground
   black pepper

¼ teaspoon crushed red pepper
   (optional)

3 cups arugula, watercress, and/or
   spinach, coarsely chopped

¼ cup pine nuts or slivered
   almonds, toasted

2 tablespoons crumbled Gorgonzola
   or other blue cheese

Start to finish: 30 minutes   Makes 4 main-dish servings

Cook pasta according to package directions. Drain. Cover and keep warm. Meanwhile, in a large skillet cook onion and garlic in hot olive oil over medium heat until onion is tender. Add tomatoes, salt, black pepper, and, if desired, red pepper. Cook and stir over medium-high heat about 2 minutes or until the tomatoes are warm and release some of their juices. Stir in arugula, watercress, or spinach and heat just until greens are wilted.

To serve, divide pasta among individual serving bowls. Top with tomato mixture. Sprinkle with toasted pine nuts or almonds and cheese.

Nutrition facts per serving: 352 cal., 11 g total fat (2 g sat. fat), 3 mg chol., 610 mg sodium, 54 g carbo., 2 g fiber, 12 g pro. Daily values: 12% vit. A, 41% vit. C, 6% calcium, 25% iron

spinach fettuccine with butter beans & tomatoes

Step into spring with this green-on-green spinach pasta tossed with fresh asparagus, butter beans, exotic mushrooms, plum tomatoes, and red onion. Serve it with a dry white wine, such as a Pinot Grigio, and focaccia or crusty Italian bread.

- 8 ounces asparagus spears, bias-sliced 1½ inches thick (1½ cups)
- 1 cup sliced fresh mushrooms (such as brown, oyster, and/or shiitake)
- ½ of a small red onion, cut into thin wedges (about ½ cup)
- 3 cloves garlic, minced
- 2 tablespoons olive oil
- 1 15-ounce can butter beans or white kidney (cannellini) beans, rinsed and drained
- 2 plum tomatoes, seeded and chopped
- ¼ cup dry white wine
- 1 9-ounce package refrigerated spinach fettuccine
- ⅓ cup freshly grated or finely shredded Asiago or Parmesan cheese

Start to finish: 25 minutes   Makes 4 main-dish servings

In a large skillet cook asparagus, mushrooms, onion, and garlic in hot olive oil for 4 to 5 minutes or just until vegetables are tender. Stir in butter beans or kidney beans, tomatoes, and white wine; heat through.

Meanwhile, cook pasta according to package directions. Drain. Return pasta to hot pan. Add bean mixture to cooked pasta; toss gently to combine. Sprinkle individual servings with cheese.

Nutrition facts per serving: 379 cal., 12 g total fat (1 g sat. fat), 19 mg chol., 303 mg sodium, 54 g carbo., 7 g fiber, 19 g pro. Daily values: 6% vit. A, 32% vit. C, 11% calcium, 18% iron

wine & dine
Consider these particularly compatible food and wine pairings:

White Table Wines	Suggested Foods
Chardonnay (dry; medium to full-bodied)	Seafood, pork, tuna, chicken
Pinot Grigio (dry; light-bodied)	Seafood, fish, poultry, antipasto
Riesling (dry to sweet; light-bodied)	Light chicken dishes
Sauvignon Blanc (dry and crisp; light- to medium-bodied)	Goat cheese, seafood

Red Table Wines	Suggested Foods
Cabernet Sauvignon (rich, dry; medium- to full-bodied)	Game, beef dishes, steak
Merlot (dry; light- to full-bodied)	Lamb, strong cheeses, steak,
Pinot Noir (smooth; light-bodied)	Salmon, strong cheeses
Zinfandel (fruity; light- to strong-bodied)	Steak, pizza, pasta dishes

rice stick & mixed vegetable stir-fry

Craving veggies? Then reap the healthy goodness of this crisp, colorful, and completely vegetarian stir-fry. Tahini paste (sesame butter) makes a delicious, nutty-tasting sauce. Look for it at Middle Eastern groceries and health food stores.

Start to finish: 30 minutes   Makes 4 main-dish servings

Soak the rice sticks in enough warm water to cover for 10 to 15 minutes or until pliable. Drain and set aside. Cut any large carrots in half lengthwise. Trim veins from leaves of bok choy; slice bok choy.

In a large skillet or wok heat cooking and sesame oils over medium-high heat. Add carrots, garlic, and gingerroot and stir-fry for 2 minutes. Add bok choy and broccoli and stir-fry for 2 minutes. Add pea pods and stir-fry for 1 to 2 minutes more or until vegetables are crisp-tender. Add tahini paste, soy sauce, and red pepper. Stir ingredients together to coat.

Spoon the vegetable mixture over rice sticks. Sprinkle with green onions and peanuts.

Nutrition facts per serving: 423 cal., 14 g total fat (2 g sat. fat), 0 mg chol., 702 mg sodium, 61 g carbo., 8 g fiber, 15 g pro. Daily values: 174% vit. A, 163% vit. C, 11% calcium, 27% iron

6 ounces dried rice sticks, broken

2 cups packaged peeled baby carrots or small carrots with tops

2 stalks bok choy

1 tablespoon cooking oil

2 teaspoons toasted sesame oil

2 garlic cloves, coarsely chopped

1 tablespoon grated gingerroot

2 cups broccoli florets

2 cups pea pods

3 tablespoons tahini paste or peanut butter

3 tablespoons reduced-sodium or regular soy sauce

¼ to ½ teaspoon crushed red pepper

2 green onions, sliced

2 tablespoons unsalted peanuts, chopped

noodle knowledge

Though popular legend has said for centuries that Italian explorer Marco Polo discovered noodles in China, both countries were enjoying them concurrently. Asians eat their noodles hot, cold, steamed, stir-fried, and deep-fried. Some of the more popular types of Asian noodles include China's cellophane noodles (made from mung-bean starch), egg noodles, and rice sticks (or rice-flour noodles); and Japan's soba (made with buckwheat flour), ramen (made with wheat and eggs), and udon (from corn or wheat).

soba noodles
with spring vegetables

This Japanese-style noodle soup satisfies any time of year. For added appeal, try using reduced-sodium chicken broth and stirring in 2 teaspoons of white or yellow miso—a soybean paste used in Asian cooking to boost flavor—with the chicken.

Start to finish: 25 minutes   Makes 3 main-dish servings

In a medium saucepan combine broth, gingerroot, and soy sauce. Bring to boiling; reduce heat. Simmer, covered, for 5 minutes.

Stir in noodles and carrot. (If using whole wheat spaghetti, stir in spaghetti and cook for 6 minutes before adding carrot.) Bring to boiling; reduce heat. Simmer, uncovered, about 4 minutes or until noodles and carrot are tender. Stir in chicken, bok choy, pea pods, radishes, and sesame oil. Heat through. Top individual servings with green onion.

Nutrition facts per serving: 276 cal., 8 g total fat (2 g sat. fat), 39 mg chol., 1,092 mg sodium, 37 g carbo., 3 g fiber, 22 g pro. Daily values: 61% vit. A, 41% vit. C, 5% calcium, 18% iron

- 1 14½-ounce can vegetable or chicken broth
- 1 tablespoon finely chopped gingerroot
- 1 tablespoon reduced-sodium soy sauce
- 4 ounces dried soba (buckwheat) noodles or whole wheat spaghetti, broken
- 1 medium carrot, thinly sliced
- 1 cup cubed cooked chicken or turkey
- 1 cup shredded bok choy
- ½ cup halved pea pods
- ⅓ cup sliced radishes or chopped daikon
- ½ teaspoon toasted sesame oil
- Green onion strips

sesame-ginger shrimp with vermicelli

The slight spiciness in this recipe comes from a healthy dose of ginger, the nuttiness from toasted sesame oil. When buying sesame oil, be sure to buy amber-colored Asian, or toasted, sesame oil—used for flavoring—rather than the lighter-colored cooking oil.

8 ounces dried vermicelli

2 tablespoons peanut oil or cooking oil

1 tablespoon grated gingerroot

2 or 3 cloves garlic, minced

1 medium yellow onion, thinly sliced

3 cups sliced fresh shiitake mushrooms (8 ounces)

2 red, green, and/or yellow sweet peppers, cut into thin strips

12 ounces peeled and deveined medium shrimp

2 tablespoons tamari sauce or reduced-sodium soy sauce

1 teaspoon finely shredded lime peel

2 tablespoons lime juice

2 teaspoons toasted sesame oil

1 teaspoon sesame seed, toasted

Start to finish: 30 minutes   Makes 4 main-dish servings

Cook pasta according to package directions. Drain. Meanwhile, in a wok or large skillet heat 1 tablespoon of the peanut or cooking oil over medium-high heat. Add gingerroot and garlic and stir-fry for 30 seconds. Add onion and stir-fry for 1 minute. Add mushrooms and peppers and stir-fry for 3 to 4 minutes more or until vegetables are crisp-tender. Remove vegetables from wok.

Add the remaining 1 tablespoon peanut oil to wok. Add shrimp and stir-fry for 2 to 3 minutes or until shrimp turn pink. Return vegetables to wok; add tamari or soy sauce, lime peel, lime juice, and sesame oil. Stir ingredients together to coat; heat through.

Divide pasta among dinner plates. Top with the shrimp mixture. Sprinkle with sesame seed.

Nutrition facts per serving: 418 cal., 12 g total fat (2 g sat. fat), 131 mg chol., 657 mg sodium, 54 g carbo., 2 g fiber, 25 g pro. Daily values: 32% vit. A, 117% vit. C, 4% calcium, 38% iron

garlic pork with broccoli & noodles

Attention, garlic lovers! Supercharged with that aromatic allium, this pork dish features lots of crisp, matchstick-sliced vegetables and soft Chinese noodles, all glazed with a sweet and spicy sauce. Serve it with Chinese beer or iced green tea.

Start to finish: 25 minutes   Makes 4 main-dish servings

Cook noodles according to package directions. Drain. Meanwhile, preheat a large skillet or wok over medium-high heat. Add ground meat and garlic and cook until meat is no longer pink. Drain off fat. Remove meat from skillet.

Add peanut or cooking and sesame oil to skillet. Add broccoli, carrot, gingerroot, and red pepper; stir-fry for 2 minutes. Stir in broth and hoisin sauce. Cook and stir until bubbly.

Stir noodles into vegetables. Stir in cooked meat and heat through.

Nutrition facts per serving: 389 cal., 11 g total fat (3 g sat. fat), 89 mg chol., 438 mg sodium, 51 g carbo., 2 g fiber, 19 g pro. Daily values: 44% vit. A, 30% vit. C, 3% calcium, 21% iron

asian tastes

Here's a sampling of some Asian flavors beyond soy sauce:
Tamari: A slightly thicker, mellower cousin of soy sauce.
Hoisin: A sweet, tongue-tingling sauce made from fermented soybeans, molasses, vinegar, mustard, sesame seed, garlic, and chilies.
Sesame Oil: A nutty-flavored, light-colored version is used in dressings and sautés. The darker version—Asian or toasted sesame oil—has a more assertive taste and fragrance and is used primarily as a flavoring.

8	ounces fresh Chinese egg noodles or fine egg noodles
12	ounces ground pork
4	cloves garlic, minced
2	teaspoons peanut oil or cooking oil
1	teaspoon toasted sesame oil
2	cups packaged shredded broccoli (broccoli slaw mix) or chopped broccoli
1	medium carrot, cut into thin 2-inch-long strips
1	tablespoon grated gingerroot
¼	teaspoon crushed red pepper
¼	cup chicken broth
¼	cup bottled hoisin sauce

one dish means dinner

sweet potato frittata with fresh cranberry salsa

Chutney, the traditional Indian relish that adds verve to this slightly sweet salsa, contains fruit (usually mangoes or limes), vinegar, sugar, and spices combined in proportions that play up contrasting flavors: sweet, sour, spicy, and piquant.

Start to finish: 25 minutes   Makes 4 servings

For cranberry salsa, in a small saucepan combine cranberries, sugar, and water. Bring to boiling, stirring occasionally. Remove from heat. Snip any large pieces of chutney. Stir chutney and ¼ cup onion into cranberry mixture. Set aside.

In a 10-inch skillet melt margarine or butter over medium heat. Add sweet potato and ¼ cup onion. Cook, covered, for 4 to 5 minutes or until potatoes are almost tender, turning once. Sprinkle with Canadian bacon.

Pour eggs over potato mixture. Cook, uncovered, over medium heat. As the eggs begin to set, run a spatula around edge of skillet, lifting eggs so uncooked portion flows underneath. Continue cooking and lifting edges until eggs are almost set (surface will be moist). Remove from heat.

Cover and let stand for 3 to 4 minutes or until top is set. Cut into wedges. Serve with warm cranberry salsa.

Nutrition facts per serving: 359 cal., 14 g total fat (4 g sat. fat), 431 mg chol., 308 mg sodium, 43 g carbo., 4 g fiber, 16 g pro. Daily values: 120% vit. A, 30% vit. C, 6% calcium, 12% iron

- 1 cup cranberries, coarsely chopped
- ¼ cup sugar
- 1 tablespoon water
- ⅓ cup chutney
- ¼ cup chopped red onion
- 1 tablespoon margarine or butter
- 1½ cups sliced and halved peeled sweet potato
- ¼ cup chopped red onion
- 2 ounces Canadian-style bacon, chopped (about ⅓ cup)
- 8 beaten eggs

hawaiian-style barbecue pizza

Deli-roasted chicken, a bread shell, and fresh pineapple chunks make assembling this pizza a breeze. If you like your food on the hotter side, look for a spicy barbecue sauce.

1 16-ounce Italian bread shell (Boboli)

½ cup barbecue sauce

1 cup shredded pizza cheese

1 to 1½ cups deli-roasted chicken
   cut into strips or chunks
   (about ½ of a chicken)

1 cup fresh pineapple chunks*

1 papaya, peeled, seeded, and sliced

1 medium green pepper,
   cut into thin strips

¼ of a small red or yellow onion,
   thinly sliced and separated
   into rings

Prep: 20 minutes   Bake: 10 minutes   Makes 4 servings

Place bread shell on an ungreased baking sheet. Spread with barbecue sauce. Sprinkle with ½ cup of the cheese. Arrange the chicken, pineapple, papaya, green pepper, and onion on top. Sprinkle with the remaining ½ cup cheese. Bake in a 425° oven about 10 minutes or until heated through.

Nutrition facts per serving: 513 cal., 15 g total fat (4 g sat. fat), 55 mg chol., 1,040 mg sodium, 65 g carbo., 4 g fiber, 32 g pro. Daily values: 18% vit. A, 113% vit. C, 27% calcium, 22% iron

Note: To save time, buy peeled pineapple in the produce section of your supermarket. Or, use one 8-ounce can pineapple chunks, drained.

pizza party

What began as a strictly Italian dish has evolved into a universally loved medium for combining all of your favorite things in one easy-to-eat piece of pie. A fun way to entertain casually is to throw a pizza gathering where your guests get involved in layering on the ingredients. Purchased Italian bread shells or focaccia works well as a base. Offer traditional sauces and toppings plus more unique ingredients. For sauces, consider pesto, peanut sauce, salsa, refrigerated alfredo or marinara sauce, or a brushing of olive oil. Fun toppers include smoked chicken or salmon, shrimp, cooked chorizo sausage, cooked asparagus, plum tomatoes, artichoke hearts, basil leaves, oil-pack dried tomatoes, kalamata olives, blue cheese, and feta cheese. Or, offer preplanned combinations such as Hawaiian-Style Barbecue Pizza.

cheese frittata with mushrooms & dill

The fuss-free Italian frittata is far easier to make than its French cousin, the omelet. This spur-of-the-moment skillet supper is terrific with Mexicali Stuffed Zucchini (page 75) and a loaf of crusty peasant-style bread.

65

Start to finish: 25 minutes   Makes 4 servings

In a medium bowl beat together eggs, cheese, water, salt, and pepper.

In a 10-inch nonstick skillet melt margarine or butter over medium-high heat. Add mushrooms and cook for 4 to 5 minutes or until liquid evaporates. Stir in green onions, parsley, and dillweed.

Pour egg mixture over mushroom mixture. Cook, uncovered, over medium heat. As the egg mixture begins to set, run a spatula around edge of skillet, lifting egg mixture so uncooked portion flows underneath. Continue cooking and lifting edges until egg mixture is almost set (surface will be moist). Remove from heat.

Cover and let stand for 3 to 4 minutes or until top is set. Cut into wedges.

Nutrition facts per serving: 216 cal., 17 g total fat (5 g sat. fat), 331 mg chol., 332 mg sodium, 3 g carbo., 0 g fiber, 13 g pro. Daily values: 26% vit. A, 5% vit. C, 12% calcium, 11% iron

- 6 beaten eggs
- ⅓ cup shredded Gruyère or Swiss cheese
- ¼ cup water
- ¼ teaspoon salt
- ⅛ teaspoon freshly ground pepper
- 2 tablespoons margarine or butter
- 1½ cups thinly sliced fresh mushrooms (such as shiitake, chanterelle, brown, or button mushrooms) (4 ounces)
- ¼ cup sliced green onions
- 1 tablespoon snipped fresh Italian flat-leaf parsley
- 1 tablespoon snipped fresh dillweed

white bean soup
with sausage & kale

Tuscan cuisine influences this earthy soup, with white beans and Italian sausage. Tomatoes and deep green kale add provincial freshness. Serve it with hearty Italian bread and, for dessert, Chocolate Ricotta-Filled Pears (page 93).

12 ounces fresh mild Italian sausage links, pricked with a fork

1 medium onion, chopped

2 cloves garlic, minced

1 tablespoon cooking oil

2 15-ounce cans white kidney (cannellini) beans, rinsed and drained

2 14½-ounce cans reduced-sodium chicken broth

1 cup seeded and coarsely chopped plum tomatoes (3 or 4 tomatoes)

1½ teaspoons snipped fresh marjoram or ½ teaspoon dried marjoram, crushed

7½ cups kale* or spinach, coarsely chopped (10 to 12 ounces)

Start to finish: 35 minutes   Makes 5 servings

In a large skillet combine sausage and ¼ cup water. Bring to boiling; reduce heat. Simmer, covered, about 15 minutes or until sausage is no longer pink. Uncover and cook about 5 minutes more or until sausage is browned, turning frequently. Remove sausage; cut into ¼- to ⅜-inch-thick slices.

Meanwhile, in a large saucepan cook onion and garlic in hot oil about 5 minutes or until onion is tender. Stir in beans, broth, tomatoes, and dried marjoram (if using). Bring to boiling; reduce heat. Simmer, covered, for 15 minutes.

Stir in cooked sausage, kale or spinach, and fresh marjoram (if using). Simmer about 5 minutes more or until kale or spinach is tender. Season to taste with pepper.

Nutrition facts per serving: 282 cal., 11 g total fat (5 g sat. fat), 39 mg chol., 1,202 mg sodium, 31 g carbo., 10 g fiber, 23 g pro. Daily values: 41% vit. A, 52% vit. C, 8% calcium, 22% iron

Note: Kale has frilly, dark green leaves and a mild cabbagelike flavor, which make it a tasty and striking addition to soups and salads.

mushroom medley soup

If you're used to mushroom soup from a can, you're in for a tasty surprise. You can prepare this soup conveniently. For speed, use presliced button mushrooms from the produce aisle of your market; if you have the time, select a variety of fresh mushrooms.

2 medium onions, cut up

2 large cloves garlic

2 medium carrots, cut up

2 tablespoons olive oil

6 cups sliced fresh mushrooms*
   (about 1 pound)

6 cups chicken broth

1 7½-ounce can tomatoes, undrained
   and cut up

2 bay leaves

2 fresh summer savory sprigs

¾ cup dried orzo pasta (rosamarina)**

2 cups shredded cooked chicken

¼ cup shredded Parmesan cheese

¼ cup snipped fresh Italian
   flat-leaf parsley

Prep: 20 minutes   Cook: 18 minutes   Makes 6 to 8 servings

In a food processor bowl combine onions and garlic. Cover and process until finely chopped. Remove from bowl. Repeat with carrots until finely chopped. (Or, finely chop vegetables by hand.)

In a 4-quart Dutch oven heat olive oil over medium heat. Add onion mixture, carrots, and mushrooms. Cook about 5 minutes or until tender. Add chicken broth, undrained tomatoes, bay leaves, and savory. Bring to boiling. Stir in pasta; reduce heat. Simmer, covered, for 10 to 12 minutes or until pasta is tender but still firm, stirring occasionally. Stir in chicken; heat through. Remove bay leaves and savory sprigs. Season to taste with salt and pepper.

Sprinkle individual servings with Parmesan cheese and parsley.

Nutrition facts per serving: 296 cal., 12 g total fat (2 g sat. fat), 49 mg chol., 971 mg sodium, 22 g carbo., 3 g fiber, 26 g pro. Daily values: 58% vit. A, 22% vit. C, 7% calcium, 24% iron

*Note: Choose from button, shiitake, brown, porcini, oyster, and/or baby portobello mushrooms.
**Note: Orzo or rosamarina (a tiny pasta that looks like long grains of rice) is ideal for soups or as a side dish in place of rice. If you like, you may substitute dried tiny bow-tie or ditalini pasta.

sea bass chowder

This delicious potage redefines chowder. It may be simple, but there is nothing plain about it. Fennel, leeks, asparagus, and fresh tomatoes join new potatoes as essential ingredients in this seafood soup.

Start to finish: 30 minutes   Makes 4 servings

Rinse fish; pat dry. Cut fish into 1-inch pieces. Set aside. Remove and snip tops from fennel; reserve for garnish. Trim the fennel bulb; cut crosswise into ¼-inch-thick slices. Chop the white and light green parts of the leek.

In a large saucepan heat oil over medium heat. Add fennel slices and leek and cook for 5 minutes. Stir in chicken broth and potatoes. Bring to boiling; reduce heat. Simmer, covered, about 10 minutes or until potatoes are tender. Stir in fish, asparagus, and pepper. Return just to boiling; reduce heat. Simmer, covered, for 2 to 3 minutes more or until fish flakes easily with a fork. Stir in tomatoes and basil.

Sprinkle individual servings with fennel tops.

Nutrition facts per serving: 223 cal., 6 g total fat (1 g sat. fat), 36 mg chol., 412 mg sodium, 22 g carbo., 9 g fiber, 21 g pro. Daily values: 11% vit. A, 56% vit. C, 4% calcium, 15% iron

12	ounces skinless fresh sea bass or grouper fillets
1	fennel bulb
1	leek
1	tablespoon cooking oil
1	14½-ounce can chicken broth
8	ounces whole tiny new potatoes, quartered
4	ounces asparagus spears, cut into 1-inch pieces
⅛	teaspoon pepper
2	large tomatoes, seeded and chopped
1	teaspoon snipped fresh basil

the fresh taste of fennel

Fresh, crisp fennel—a member of the anise family—is enjoyed for its light, licoricelike flavor. When this plant is cooked, the licorice flavor becomes more subtle. The tops often are used for seasoning in salads and soups.

Fennel is available September through April. Look for firm, smooth bulbs without cracks or brown spots. The stalks should be crisp, the leaves green and fresh. Store fennel in a plastic bag in the refrigerator for up to 4 days.

bacon & dried tomato risotto

No doubt about it—hickory-smoked bacon and tomato have a real affinity (just ask any BLT aficionado). Here, the two companions pair up with green onions and parsley, with a little sweet corn tossed in, to make risotto with an American accent.

70

2	cups reduced-sodium chicken broth
1½	cups water
2	tablespoons margarine or butter
1¼	cups uncooked arborio rice or other short-grain rice
1	cup frozen whole kernel corn
¼	cup finely snipped dried tomatoes (not oil-packed)
½	cup dry white wine or water
6	green onions, thinly sliced
4	slices bacon, crisp-cooked, drained, and crumbled
3	tablespoons grated Parmesan or Romano cheese
3	tablespoons snipped fresh parsley

Start to finish: 30 minutes   Makes 4 servings

In a medium saucepan bring the chicken broth and water to boiling; reduce heat. Simmer until needed. Meanwhile, in a large saucepan melt margarine or butter over medium heat. Add rice; cook and stir for 30 seconds.

Slowly add 1 cup of the hot broth mixture to rice, stirring constantly. Continue to cook and stir until liquid is absorbed. Add another ½ cup of the broth mixture, the corn, and dried tomatoes, stirring constantly. Continue to cook and stir until liquid is absorbed. Add the remaining broth mixture (½ cup at a time), continuing to cook and stir until liquid is absorbed (this should take about 15 minutes).

Stir in the wine. Cook and stir just until the rice is tender and slightly creamy. Stir in green onions, bacon, Parmesan or Romano cheese, and parsley. Season to taste with freshly ground pepper.

Nutrition facts per serving: 407 cal., 12 g total fat (3 g sat. fat), 9 mg chol., 653 mg sodium, 61 g carbo., 0 g fiber, 11 g pro. Daily values: 14% vit. A, 20% vit. C, 7% calcium, 22% iron

take-it-easy paella

The national dish of Spain just got simple enough to make in less than 30 minutes! Lean sausage, shrimp, tomatoes, and peas stud this version of the saffron rice. Serve it with a dry Spanish white wine.

Prep: 10 minutes Cook: 17 minutes   Makes 4 servings

In a large skillet combine sausage, leeks, chicken broth, rice, water, dried thyme (if using), saffron, and red pepper. Bring to boiling; reduce heat. Simmer, covered, about 15 minutes or just until rice is tender.

Stir in shrimp, tomatoes, peas, and fresh thyme (if using). Cook and stir gently for 2 to 3 minutes more or until heated through.

Nutrition facts per serving: 377 cal., 6 g total fat (1 g sat. fat), 147 mg chol., 935 mg sodium, 51 g carbo., 4 g fiber, 29 g pro. Daily values: 9% vit. A, 29% vit. C, 9% calcium, 41% iron

super **sippers**

All of the recipes in this book feature fresh, lively flavors, so it's only fitting that you'd want to offer a refreshing beverage that's on a par with whatever you're serving. Consider some of these ideas:

- Sparkling water with fruit juice ice cubes (orange, cranberry, mango, or papaya, for instance) and fresh mint sprigs.
- Cranberry spritzers made with cranberry juice, sparkling water, and a twist of fresh lime.
- Flavored iced teas, such as herbal tea or raspberry- or currant-flavored black tea.

8 ounces cooked smoked turkey sausage, halved lengthwise and cut into ½-inch pieces

2 leeks, sliced ¼ inch thick

1 14½-ounce can reduced-sodium chicken broth

1 cup uncooked long-grain rice

½ cup water

1 tablespoon snipped fresh thyme or 1 teaspoon dried thyme, crushed

¼ teaspoon ground saffron

⅛ to ¼ teaspoon ground red pepper

8 ounces peeled cooked shrimp

3 plum tomatoes, seeded and chopped

1 cup frozen peas

swift sides

roasted vegetables
with balsamic vinegar

Roasting brings out the natural sweetness of vegetables. These earthy and elegant roasted green beans and summer squash balance just about any entrée—steaks, chicken, pork chops, or salmon.

Start to finish: 25 minutes   Makes 4 to 6 servings

In a shallow roasting pan combine beans, onion, and garlic. Drizzle with olive oil; sprinkle with salt and pepper. Toss mixture until beans are evenly coated. Spread into a single layer.

Roast in a 450° oven for 8 minutes. Stir in squash and roast for 5 to 7 minutes more or until vegetables are tender and slightly browned.

Meanwhile, in a small saucepan bring the balsamic vinegar to boiling over medium-high heat; reduce heat. Boil gently about 5 minutes or until reduced by half (vinegar will thicken slightly).

Drizzle the vinegar over roasted vegetables; toss until vegetables are evenly coated.

Nutrition facts per serving: 81 cal., 4 g total fat (1 g sat. fat), 0 mg chol., 45 mg sodium, 12 g carbo., 1 g fiber, 1 g pro. Daily values: 4% vit. A, 19% vit. C, 3% calcium, 9% iron

8 ounces green beans, ends trimmed

1 small onion, cut into thin wedges

1 clove garlic, minced

1 tablespoon olive oil

   Dash salt

   Dash pepper

2 medium yellow summer squash, halved lengthwise and sliced ¼ inch thick

⅓ cup balsamic vinegar

vegetable risotto

The beauty of this risotto is its adaptability (use any vegetable in season) and its ease (check out the super-simple alternate method). Try Vegetable Risotto as a side for Pork Medallions with Fennel & Pancetta (page 27).

3 cups chicken or vegetable broth

1 medium onion, chopped

2 cloves garlic, minced

2 tablespoons olive oil or cooking oil

1 cup uncooked arborio rice or other short-grain rice

2 cups vegetables (such as ½-inch pieces of asparagus or broccoli, sliced carrots, halved pea pods, chopped winter squash, sliced summer squash, or peas)

½ cup shredded spinach

3 tablespoons grated Parmesan cheese

Start to finish: 35 minutes   Makes 6 servings

In a medium saucepan bring the chicken or vegetable broth to boiling; reduce heat. Simmer until needed. Meanwhile, in a large saucepan cook onion and garlic in hot oil until onion is tender. Add rice; cook and stir over medium heat about 5 minutes or until rice is golden brown.

Slowly add 1 cup of the hot broth to the rice mixture, stirring constantly. Continue to cook and stir until liquid is absorbed. Add another 1 cup of the broth (½ cup at a time), continuing to cook and stir until the liquid is absorbed. Add the 2 cups vegetables and another ½ cup broth, continuing to cook and stir until liquid is absorbed (this should take about 15 minutes). Stir in remaining broth. Cook and stir just until rice is tender and slightly creamy. Stir in spinach and cheese.

Nutrition facts per serving: 208 cal., 6 g total fat (1 g sat. fat), 3 mg chol., 463 mg sodium, 30 g carbo., 2 g fiber, 7 g pro. Daily values: 33% vit. A, 32% vit. C, 6% calcium, 15% iron

Easy Vegetable Risotto: Cook onion and garlic in hot oil until tender. Add rice; cook and stir over medium heat about 5 minutes or until golden. Stir in broth. Bring to boiling; reduce heat. Simmer, covered, for 10 minutes. Stir in the 2 cups vegetables and cook for 10 minutes more. Remove from heat. Let stand, covered, for 5 minutes. If necessary, stir in a little water to make slightly creamy. Stir in spinach and cheese.

mexicali stuffed zucchini

These savory stuffed zucchini "wheels" can be made a day ahead: Prepare them up to the baking step; then cover the dish with plastic wrap and chill. About 25 minutes before serving, simply remove the wrap and bake.

Prep: 25 minutes   Bake: 21 minutes   Makes 5 or 6 servings

Cut zucchini into 1½-inch rounds. Scoop out the pulp, leaving ¼- to ½-inch-thick shells. Chop enough of the pulp to make ⅓ cup. In a medium skillet cook garlic in hot oil over medium-high heat for 1 minute. Add the reserved zucchini pulp, the sweet red pepper, green onions, 1 tablespoon of the cilantro, and the jalapeño pepper. Cook and stir about 2 minutes or until vegetables are crisp-tender.

Place zucchini shells in a lightly greased 2-quart rectangular baking dish. Fill each shell with pepper mixture. Bake, uncovered, in a 350° oven for 20 to 25 minutes or until zucchini is tender. Sprinkle with cheese and bake for 1 to 2 minutes more or until cheese melts.

Sprinkle with the remaining 1 tablespoon cilantro. Serve with the Cucumber Raita.

Cucumber Raita: In a small bowl combine ½ cup plain low-fat yogurt, ¼ cup peeled and finely chopped cucumber, 1 tablespoon snipped fresh cilantro, and ⅛ teaspoon salt.

Nutrition facts per serving: 101 cal., 6 g total fat (3 g sat. fat), 11 mg chol., 135 mg sodium, 9 g carbo., 2 g fiber, 5 g pro. Daily values: 19% vit. A, 62% vit. C, 12% calcium, 4% iron

3 medium zucchini, ends trimmed (about 1¾ pounds)

2 cloves garlic, minced

2 teaspoons cooking oil

1 medium red sweet pepper, chopped

3 green onions, thinly sliced

2 tablespoons snipped fresh cilantro

1 fresh or canned jalapeño pepper, seeded and finely chopped

½ cup shredded Monterey Jack cheese (2 ounces)

1 recipe Cucumber Raita

corn cakes with fresh corn & chives

Everything old is new again! That most traditional of American foods, the corn cake, has been updated with fresh corn and just-snipped herbs. Try them with Tenderloin Steaks with Arugula-Cornichon Relish (page 19).

1 fresh ear of corn or ½ cup frozen whole kernel corn

2 tablespoons all-purpose flour

1½ teaspoons baking powder

1 teaspoon sugar

½ teaspoon salt

1 cup boiling water

1 cup yellow cornmeal

¼ cup milk

1 slightly beaten egg

1 tablespoon snipped fresh chives

3 tablespoons cooking oil

1 teaspoon snipped fresh chives or cilantro (optional)

⅓ cup dairy sour cream

Prep: 20 minutes Cook: 6 minutes Makes 6 servings

Cut corn kernels from cob and measure ½ cup. In a small bowl combine flour, baking powder, sugar, and salt. Set aside.

In a medium bowl stir boiling water into cornmeal to make a stiff mush. Stir in milk until smooth; then stir in fresh or frozen corn, egg, and the 1 tablespoon chives. Add flour mixture and stir just until combined.

In a large skillet heat 2 tablespoons of the oil over medium heat. Drop batter by rounded tablespoons into hot oil. Cook for 3 to 4 minutes or until golden brown, turning once. Transfer to a serving platter; cover and keep warm. Repeat with remaining batter, adding the remaining 1 tablespoon oil.

Meanwhile, stir the 1 teaspoon chives, if desired, into sour cream. Serve with the corn cakes.

Nutrition facts per serving: 215 cal., 11 g total fat (3 g sat. fat), 42 mg chol., 295 mg sodium, 25 g carbo., 2 g fiber, 4 g pro. Daily values: 6% vit. A, 2% vit. C, 10% calcium, 9% iron

potato-leek pancakes

Potato pancakes with applesauce used to be a stand-alone Sunday night supper. Leeks, sour cream, parsley, and Parmesan cheese flavor these crisp coins of shredded potatoes. Try them with roasted chicken, grilled sausages, or a salad.

78

3 **large baking potatoes
     (about 1¼ pounds total)**

2 **leeks, very thinly sliced (white
     and light green parts only)**

2 **slightly beaten eggs**

¼ **cup grated Parmesan cheese**

3 **tablespoons all-purpose flour**

2 **tablespoons snipped fresh parsley**

2 **tablespoons dairy sour cream**

⅛ **teaspoon salt**

⅛ **teaspoon pepper**

1 **tablespoon cooking oil**

Prep: 15 minutes Cook: 16 minutes   Makes 6 servings

Coarsely shred unpeeled potatoes in a food processor. Pat dry with paper towels. In a large bowl combine potatoes, leeks, eggs, Parmesan cheese, flour, parsley, sour cream, salt, and pepper.

In a large skillet heat the oil over medium heat. For each pancake, drop about ¼ cup potato mixture into the hot oil and press each pancake gently with a spatula to flatten it to uniform thickness (cook 6 pancakes at a time).

Cook for 8 to 10 minutes or until crisp and brown, turning once when the edges brown. Remove from skillet. Repeat with remaining potato mixture.

Nutrition facts per serving: 219 cal., 9 g total fat (4 g sat. fat), 82 mg chol., 164 mg sodium, 28 g carbo., 2 g fiber, 7 g pro. Daily values: 9% vit. A, 27% vit. C, 9% calcium, 17% iron

fried green tomatoes on a bed of greens

This classic Southern side gets greener and tastier with the addition of mesclun, a mixture of tiny salad greens. Buy unripened green tomatoes at your market or harvest them from your garden.

Prep: 20 minutes Cook: 8 minutes   Makes 4 servings

In a pie plate or baking dish combine cornmeal, the ¼ teaspoon salt, and the ⅛ teaspoon pepper. Coat both sides of tomato slices with the cornmeal mixture. In a large skillet heat cooking or olive oil over medium heat. Add tomato slices, half at a time, and cook about 4 minutes or until golden brown, turning once. (Add more oil if necessary.) Drain on paper towels. Repeat with remaining tomato slices.

In a medium bowl drizzle the mesclun with olive oil and vinegar. Sprinkle with the salt and pepper; toss to coat.

Divide the mesclun mixture among salad plates. Top with the tomatoes.

Nutrition facts per serving: 188 cal., 15 g total fat (2 g sat. fat), 0 mg chol., 180 mg sodium, 12 g carbo., 2 g fiber, 2 g pro. Daily values: 7% vit. A, 30% vit. C, 1% calcium, 7% iron

¼ cup yellow cornmeal

¼ teaspoon salt

⅛ teaspoon freshly ground pepper

2 large green tomatoes, sliced about ⅜ inch thick (8 center-cut slices)

3 tablespoons cooking oil or olive oil

4 cups mesclun

4 teaspoons olive oil

2 teaspoons balsamic vinegar

   Dash salt

   Dash pepper

pear & endive salad with honey-walnut vinaigrette

Made with pears and embellished with crunchy walnuts, this endive salad is ideal with Rosemary Pork Chop Skillet (page 25). Start the salad while the chops are simmering, add some bakery bread, then settle in for an earthy but elegant dinner.

Prep: 20 minutes   Makes 4 servings

In a small bowl gently toss pear or apple slices with lemon juice to prevent darkening. Place the endive leaves in salad bowls or salad plates; top with the sliced pears or apples. Sprinkle with walnuts, salt, and pepper.

For vinaigrette, in a small bowl combine olive or salad oil, sherry or white wine vinegar, shallot or onion, honey, and cinnamon; whisk until thoroughly blended.

Drizzle the vinaigrette over the salads. If desired, sprinkle with pomegranate seeds.

Nutrition facts per serving: 216 cal., 15 g total fat (2 g sat. fat), 0 mg chol., 39 mg sodium, 22 g carbo., 3 g fiber, 2 g pro. Daily values: 3% vit. A, 21% vit. C, 1% calcium, 6% iron

2 ripe red Bartlett pears, Bosc pears, and/or apples, cored and thinly sliced

2 tablespoons lemon juice

8 ounces Belgian endive, leaves separated (2 medium heads)

¼ cup coarsely chopped walnuts

Dash salt

Dash pepper

3 tablespoons olive oil or salad oil

2 tablespoons sherry vinegar or white wine vinegar

1 shallot, finely chopped, or 1 tablespoon finely chopped onion

1 tablespoon honey

½ teaspoon ground cinnamon

Pomegranate seeds (optional)

orange & new potato salad

What will you do with that jar of jalapeño jelly recently bestowed by your best friend? Quit wondering. Use the sweet-and-fiery condiment as the secret zing in this new potato salad that's great with grilled foods.

2 oranges

1 pound whole tiny new potatoes, sliced

1 shallot, finely chopped

2 tablespoons cooking oil

2 tablespoons jalapeño jelly

2 tablespoons white wine vinegar

½ of a small red onion, thinly sliced and separated into rings

Leaf lettuce (optional)

2 tablespoons snipped fresh chives (optional)

Prep: 15 minutes Cook: 10 minutes Chill: 1 hour
Makes 4 to 6 servings

Finely shred 1 teaspoon orange peel; set aside. Peel oranges; then halve lengthwise and slice; set aside. In a large covered saucepan cook the potatoes in a small amount of boiling, lightly salted water about 10 minutes or just until tender. Drain in colander. Rinse with cold water; drain again.

Meanwhile, in a small saucepan cook shallot in hot oil for 3 minutes. Stir in jelly and vinegar. Cook and stir until jelly is melted. Stir in reserved orange peel. In a medium bowl combine cooked potatoes, orange slices, and onion. Pour jelly mixture over potato mixture; toss to coat. Cover and refrigerate for 1 to 24 hours.

To serve, if desired, spoon potato mixture onto a lettuce-lined platter and sprinkle with chives.

Nutrition facts per serving: 222 cal., 7 g total fat (1 g sat. fat), 0 mg chol., 13 mg sodium, 38 g carbo., 2 g fiber, 3 g pro. Daily values: 8% vit. A, 57% vit. C, 3% calcium, 15% iron

beet & watercress salad

Don't banish beets to the borscht pot! Tender and very sweet baby beets contrast beautifully with the spicy watercress in this enticing salad. Top it with a minty sour-cream dressing and toasted walnuts.

Prep: 25 minutes Cook: 15 minutes Chill: 1 hour   Makes 4 servings

Trim tops of baby beets to ½ inch. Or, trim tops and roots of medium beets to 1 inch on each end. In a covered medium saucepan cook beets with the rosemary sprig in a small amount of boiling salted water about 15 minutes (about 30 minutes for medium beets) or until tender. Drain and cool slightly.

Slip off skins of beets. If using medium beets, cut each beet into 6 wedges. Cover and refrigerate for 1 to 24 hours. For dressing, in a small bowl combine sour cream, mint, and honey. Cover and refrigerate.

To serve, place the watercress leaves on salad plates. Top with chilled beets. Spoon the dressing over salads and sprinkle with toasted walnuts.

Nutrition facts per serving: 112 cal., 8 g total fat (2 g sat. fat), 6 mg chol., 45 mg sodium, 9 g carbo., 3 g fiber, 3 g pro. Daily values: 12% vit. A, 19% vit. C, 4% calcium, 6% iron

20 red, yellow, and/or candy stripe baby beets or 3 medium beets (12 ounces)

 1 fresh rosemary sprig

¼ cup dairy sour cream

 1 tablespoon snipped fresh mint

 2 teaspoons honey

 2 cups watercress leaves

¼ cup broken walnuts, toasted

fresh &
simple finales

gingered shortcake with spiced fruit

Shortcake isn't just for summer berries anymore! Enjoy this warming dessert with fall fruits such as apples, persimmons, or pears. The shortcake can be made ahead and refrigerated, then warmed—wrapped in foil—in a 350° oven about 25 minutes.

Prep: 25 minutes Bake: 18 minutes Cool: 40 minutes
Makes 8 servings

Prepare Gingered Shortcake. In a chilled bowl combine cream, granulated sugar, and vanilla. Beat with chilled beaters of an electric mixer until soft peaks form. Cover and refrigerate. In a large skillet melt butter over medium heat. Add apples, persimmons, and/or pears. Cook for 2 to 5 minutes or until almost tender. Stir in brown sugar and nutmeg. Cook for 1 to 3 minutes more or until fruit is tender. Stir in blueberries.

Place bottom cake layer on serving plate. Spoon about two-thirds of the fruit mixture and half of the whipped cream over cake. Top with second cake layer and remaining fruit mixture. Pass remaining whipped cream.

Gingered Shortcake: Combine 2 cups all-purpose flour, ¼ cup granulated sugar, and 2 teaspoons baking powder. Cut in ½ cup butter until mixture resembles coarse crumbs. Combine 1 beaten egg, ⅔ cup milk, and 1 tablespoon grated gingerroot; add to dry mixture. Stir just to moisten. Spread in a greased 8×1½-inch round baking pan. Bake in a 450° oven for 18 to 20 minutes or until a wooden toothpick inserted near center comes out clean. Cool in pan for 10 minutes. Remove from pan; cool on a wire rack for 30 minutes. Split into 2 layers.

Nutrition facts per serving: 457 cal., 28 g total fat (17 g sat. fat), 111 mg chol., 280 mg sodium, 47 g carbo., 2 g fiber, 5 g pro. Daily values: 30% vit. A, 6% vit. C, 12% calcium, 11% iron

- 1 **recipe Gingered Shortcake**
- 1 **cup whipping cream**
- 2 **tablespoons granulated sugar**
- ½ **teaspoon vanilla**
- 3 **tablespoons butter**
- 3 **medium cooking apples, Fuyu persimmons, and/or pears, cored (if necessary) and thinly sliced**
- 3 **tablespoons brown sugar**
- ¼ **teaspoon ground nutmeg**
- 1 **cup blueberries**

apple-berry "pie"

A bit like a pie (though far easier to make) and a bit like a cobbler—that's the fun of this homey baked fruit dessert. Serve it slightly warm and top it with a scoop of vanilla ice cream or a spoonful of cream. Your guests will eat it with gusto!

1 pound apples, quartered and cored (about 3 medium)

1 cup cranberries

¼ cup walnuts

½ cup sugar

¼ cup raisins

1 tablespoon finely shredded orange peel

1 egg

½ cup all-purpose flour

½ cup butter, melted

⅓ cup sugar

1½ teaspoons finely shredded orange peel

½ teaspoon vanilla

⅛ teaspoon salt

Several drops almond extract

Prep: 20 minutes Bake: 40 minutes   Makes 8 servings

Generously butter a 9-inch pie plate; set aside. Place unpeeled apples in a food processor bowl. Cover and process until coarsely chopped. Remove from bowl. Repeat with the cranberries until coarsely chopped, then the walnuts. (Or, coarsely chop ingredients by hand.) In a medium bowl combine apples, cranberries, walnuts, the ½ cup sugar, the raisins, and the 1 tablespoon orange peel. Spread mixture evenly in the bottom of pie plate.

For topping, in the food processor bowl or a mixing bowl combine egg, flour, melted butter, the ⅓ cup sugar, the 1½ teaspoons orange peel, the vanilla, salt, and almond extract. Cover and process or beat with an electric mixer until smooth. Spread batter evenly over fruit mixture.

Bake in a 350° oven about 40 minutes or until topping is browned and a toothpick inserted in the center comes out clean. Cool slightly and serve warm*.

Nutrition facts per serving: 290 cal., 15 g total fat (8 g sat. fat), 57 mg chol., 159 mg sodium, 40 g carbo., 2 g fiber, 2 g pro. Daily values: 12% vit. A, 9% vit. C, 1% calcium, 4% iron

*Note: To make the "pie" ahead, bake as directed and cool completely. Cover with foil and refrigerate for up to 24 hours. To reheat, bake, covered, in a 350° oven about 20 minutes or until warm.

espresso-orange sauce

Italians may drink their espresso in an express fashion at coffee bars and train stations, but you can savor this ice-cream sauce featuring the famed Italian coffee. If your market carries them, use sweet, juicy, cabernet-colored blood oranges.

87

Start to finish: 20 minutes   Makes 16 servings

Using a vegetable peeler, cut a few strips of peel from 1 of the oranges. Cut the strips into very thin strips and place in a small bowl of water. Cover and refrigerate. Peel the oranges. Halve oranges lengthwise and slice; set aside.

In a medium saucepan combine the brown sugar and cornstarch. Stir in water, espresso powder, and stick cinnamon. Cook and stir over medium heat until thickened and bubbly. Cook and stir for 2 minutes more. Remove from heat. Remove stick cinnamon. Stir in orange slices and, if desired, liqueur.

Drain the orange strips. Serve the sauce warm or cool over ice cream. Sprinkle with the orange strips and almonds.

Nutrition facts per serving (with ice cream): 106 cal., 5 g total fat (2 g sat. fat), 15 mg chol., 28 mg sodium, 14 g carbo., 1 g fiber, 2 g pro. Daily values: 4% vit. A, 7% vit. C, 5% calcium, 2% iron

2 oranges
⅓ cup packed brown sugar
4 teaspoons cornstarch
1 cup water
1 tablespoon instant espresso coffee powder
2 inches stick cinnamon
1 tablespoon coffee liqueur (optional)
   Vanilla ice cream
   Sliced almonds, toasted, or honey-roasted almonds

almond cookie cups with sorbet

Like pastel eggs in an Easter basket, scoops of sorbet are nestled prettily in crisp, almond-flavored cups. In addition to raspberry and lemon sorbet, try other flavors, such as lime, grapefruit, peach, and pear.

1 cup all-purpose flour

1 cup sliced almonds, finely chopped

¾ cup packed dark brown sugar

½ cup light-colored corn syrup

½ cup butter

1 teaspoon vanilla

3 cups raspberry and/or lemon sorbet

   Fresh raspberries

Prep: 15 minutes Bake: 10 minutes per batch   Makes 6 servings

In a small bowl combine the flour and almonds; set aside. In a medium saucepan bring the brown sugar, corn syrup, and butter to a full boil over medium heat. Remove from heat. Stir in the flour mixture and vanilla.

Line a large cookie sheet with parchment paper. For each cookie cup, drop about 3 tablespoonfuls of batter about 5 inches apart onto prepared cookie sheet (bake 3 or 4 at a time). Bake in a 350° oven for 10 to 12 minutes or until bubbly and deep golden brown (cookies will form irregular shapes). Let stand on cookie sheet about 2 minutes. When cookies are firm but still pliable, place them on top of inverted custard cups to form small bowls. Cool to room temperature.

To serve, fill 6 of the cups with scoops of raspberry and/or lemon sorbet. Garnish with raspberries. Serve immediately. Store the remaining cups in an airtight container in the freezer for up to 3 months.

Nutrition facts per serving: 380 cal., 15 g total fat (6 g sat. fat), 25 mg chol., 121 mg sodium, 60 g carbo., 1 g fiber, 4 g pro. Daily values: 8% vit. A, 6% vit. C, 8% calcium, 11% iron

chilled fruit soup

Scandinavians and Hungarians enjoy fruit soup as a starter before a great feast. But—swirled with a little sweetened whipped cream—the soup is just as nice after a meal. Use any soft, ripe, seasonal fruit that strikes your fancy.

4 cups seasonal fruit (such as blueberries, raspberries, and/or cut-up cantaloupe, honeydew melon, or strawberries)

1 8-ounce carton plain low-fat yogurt

½ cup sugar

3 tablespoons lemon juice

¼ cup whipping cream

1 teaspoon sugar

Prep: 20 minutes Chill: 4 hours Makes 4 to 6 servings

In a blender container or food processor bowl combine half of the fruit, half of the yogurt, ¼ cup of the sugar, and 2 tablespoons of the lemon juice. Cover and blend or process until smooth. Strain mixture through a fine sieve into a large storage container or pitcher with a lid. Repeat with the remaining fruit, remaining yogurt, ¼ cup of the sugar, and remaining lemon juice. Combine with the first batch of fruit soup. Cover and refrigerate for 4 to 24 hours.

Before serving, in a chilled small bowl combine whipping cream and the 1 teaspoon sugar. Beat with an electric mixer on medium speed until soft peaks form.

To serve, stir fruit soup, then divide among dessert bowls. Swirl the whipped cream into individual servings.

Nutrition facts per serving: 251 cal., 7 g total fat (4 g sat. fat), 24 mg chol., 52 mg sodium, 46 g carbo., 3 g fiber, 4 g pro. Daily values: 21% vit. A, 93% vit. C, 11% calcium, 3% iron

red wine-marinated peaches

Carpe diem, meaning "seize the day" in Latin, must refer to that much-anticipated though fleeting time in late summer when juicy peaches are at their peak. Embellish this golden fruit with red wine, cinnamon, and cloves.

Prep: 15 minutes Marinate: 30 minutes   Makes 6 servings

Place peaches or pears in a large bowl. For marinade, in a medium saucepan combine the wine, sugar, cinnamon, and cloves. Cook and stir over medium heat until sugar is dissolved.

Pour the marinade over peaches; toss gently to coat. Marinate at room temperature for 30 to 60 minutes, stirring occasionally. To serve, spoon peaches and marinade into dessert dishes.

Nutrition facts per serving: 262 cal., 0 g total fat (0 g sat. fat), 0 mg chol., 6 mg sodium, 51 g carbo., 3 g fiber, 1 g pro. Daily values: 9% vit. A, 18% vit. C, 1% calcium, 2% iron

6 ripe medium peaches, peeled, pitted, and sliced, or pears, cored and sliced

1½ cups fruity red wine (such as Beaujolais) or dry white wine

¾ cup sugar

½ teaspoon ground cinnamon

⅛ teaspoon ground cloves

don't desert **dessert**

If you don't have time to make even the simplest recipe, dessert doesn't have to be a lost prospect. Try one of these super-simple dessert ideas that will satisfy the craving for just a little something sweet after a delicious dinner:

- Fresh fruit sliced and tossed with a little honey and sprinkled with toasted almonds. Ripe, juicy peaches, nectarines, or plums are great choices.
- A tea bar set up with several kinds of teabags (a selection of herbal, decaffeinated, and black tea among them), lemon, milk, honey, and sugar—and purchased tea biscuits.
- A cheese course featuring a selection of cheeses and fresh fruit. Some perfect pairings include ripe pears with a blue cheese such as Roquefort or Gorgonzola; berries and apples with brie; oranges (particularly blood oranges, which are super-juicy and sweet) with thin wedges of Parmesan or Romano.

chocolate ricotta-filled pears

Discover all the wonderful flavors of the classic Sicilian ricotta-chocolate-fruit-filled cake called *cassata*—without turning on your oven or chopping a thing. Be sure the pears are ripe. Serve them with an Italian dessert wine, such as Vin Santo.

93

Prep: 20 minutes   Makes 6 servings

In a medium bowl beat the ricotta cheese, sugar, cocoa powder, and vanilla with an electric mixer on medium speed until combined. Stir in chocolate pieces and the 1 teaspoon orange peel. Set aside.

Peel the pears; cut in half lengthwise and remove the cores. Remove a thin slice from the rounded sides so the pear halves will sit flat. Brush the pears all over with orange juice. Place the pears on dessert plates. Spoon the ricotta mixture on top of the pears and sprinkle with almonds. If desired, garnish with mint leaves and orange curls.

Nutrition facts per serving: 166 cal., 6 g total fat (2 g sat. fat), 13 mg chol., 52 mg sodium, 24 g carbo., 3 g fiber, 6 g pro. Daily values: 5% vit. A, 10% vit. C, 11% calcium, 4% iron

1 **cup ricotta cheese**

⅓ **cup sifted powdered sugar**

1 **tablespoon unsweetened cocoa powder**

¼ **teaspoon vanilla**

2 **tablespoons miniature semisweet chocolate pieces**

1 **teaspoon finely shredded orange peel**

3 **large ripe Bosc, Anjou, or Bartlett pears**

2 **tablespoons orange juice**

2 **tablespoons slivered or sliced almonds, toasted**

Fresh mint leaves (optional)

Orange peel curls (optional)

94

METRIC COOKING HINTS

By making a few conversions, cooks in Australia, Canada, and the United Kingdom can use the recipes in *Better Homes and Gardens® Fresh and Simple™ Cooking for Friends* with confidence. The charts on this page provide a guide for converting measurements from the U.S. customary system, which is used throughout this book, to the imperial and metric systems. There also is a conversion table for oven temperatures to accommodate the differences in oven calibrations.

Product Differences: Most of the ingredients called for in the recipes in this book are available in English-speaking countries. However, some are known by different names. Here are some common American ingredients and their possible counterparts:

- Sugar is granulated or castor sugar.
- Powdered sugar is icing sugar.
- All-purpose flour is plain household flour or white flour. When self-rising flour is used in place of all-purpose flour in a recipe that calls for leavening, omit the leavening agent (baking soda or baking powder) and salt.
- Light-colored corn syrup is golden syrup.
- Cornstarch is cornflour.
- Baking soda is bicarbonate of soda.
- Vanilla is vanilla essence.
- Green, red, or yellow sweet peppers are capsicums.
- Golden raisins are sultanas.

Volume and Weight: Americans traditionally use cup measures for liquid and solid ingredients. The chart, above right, shows the approximate imperial and metric equivalents. If you are accustomed to weighing solid ingredients, the following approximate equivalents will be helpful.

- 1 cup butter, castor sugar, or rice = 8 ounces = about 250 grams
- 1 cup flour = 4 ounces = about 125 grams
- 1 cup icing sugar = 5 ounces = about 150 grams

Spoon measures are used for smaller amounts of ingredients. Although the size of the tablespoon varies slightly in different countries, for practical purposes and for recipes in this book, a straight substitution is all that's necessary.

Measurements made using cups or spoons always should be level unless stated otherwise.

Equivalents: U.S. = Australia/U.K.

⅛ teaspoon = 0.5 ml
¼ teaspoon = 1 ml
½ teaspoon = 2 ml
1 teaspoon = 5 ml
1 tablespoon = 1 tablespoon
¼ cup = 2 tablespoons = 2 fluid ounces = 60 ml
⅓ cup = ¼ cup = 3 fluid ounces = 90 ml
½ cup = ⅓ cup = 4 fluid ounces = 120 ml
⅔ cup = ½ cup = 5 fluid ounces = 150 ml
¾ cup = ⅔ cup = 6 fluid ounces = 180 ml
1 cup = ¾ cup = 8 fluid ounces = 240 ml
1¼ cups = 1 cup
2 cups = 1 pint
1 quart = 1 liter
½ inch = 1.27 cm
1 inch = 2.54 cm

Baking Pan Sizes

American	Metric
8×1½-inch round baking pan	20×4-cm cake tin
9×1½-inch round baking pan	23×3.5-cm cake tin
11×7×1½-inch baking pan	28×18×4-cm baking tin
13×9×2-inch baking pan	30×20×3-cm baking tin
2-quart rectangular baking dish	30×20×3-cm baking tin
15×10×1-inch baking pan	30×25×2-cm baking tin (Swiss roll tin)
9-inch pie plate	22×4- or 23×4-cm pie plate
7- or 8-inch springform pan	18- or 20-cm springform or loose-bottom cake tin
9×5×3-inch loaf pan	23×13×7-cm or 2-pound narrow loaf tin or pâté tin
1½-quart casserole	1.5-liter casserole
2-quart casserole	2-liter casserole

Oven Temperature Equivalents

Fahrenheit Setting	Celsius Setting*	Gas Setting
300°F	150°C	Gas Mark 2 (slow)
325°F	160°C	Gas Mark 3 (moderately slow)
350°F	180°C	Gas Mark 4 (moderate)
375°F	190°C	Gas Mark 5 (moderately hot)
400°F	200°C	Gas Mark 6 (hot)
425°F	220°C	Gas Mark 7
450°F	230°C	Gas Mark 8 (very hot)
Broil		Grill

*Electric and gas ovens may be calibrated using Celsius. However, for an electric oven, increase the Celsius setting 10 to 20 degrees when cooking above 160°C. For convection or forced-air ovens (gas or electric), lower the temperature setting 10°C when cooking at all heat levels.